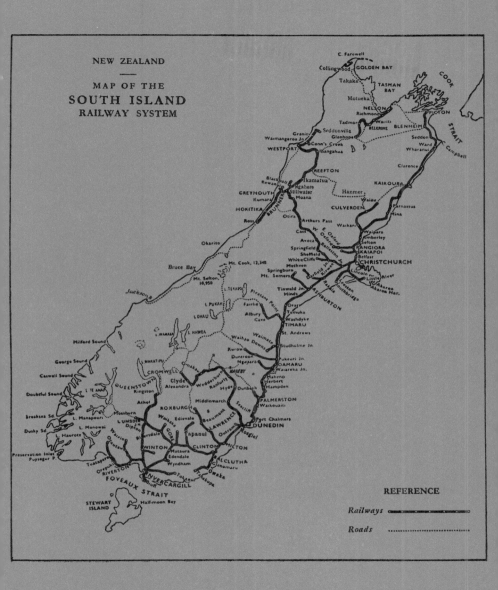

NEW ZEALAND

—

MAP OF THE
SOUTH ISLAND
RAILWAY SYSTEM

REFERENCE

Railways
Roads

Engine Pass

NEW ZEALAND RAILWAYS

ENGINE PASS
New Zealand Railways

by

D. B. LEITCH

A. H. & A. W. REED

WELLINGTON – AUCKLAND – SYDNEY

First published 1967

A. H. & A. W. REED
182 Wakefield Street, Wellington
29 Dacre Street, Auckland
51 Whiting Street, Artarmon, Sydney

Printed in 10/11 point Times Linotype
PRINTED IN AUSTRALIA BY HALSTEAD PRESS, SYDNEY

TO MY WIFE

WHO WAS A MODEL OF TOLERANCE THROUGHOUT

WITH AFFECTION

AND TO MY MANY FOOTPLATE FRIENDS

IN APPRECIATION

Contents

List of illustrations

facing page

All photographs not otherwise credited are by the author.

Acknowledgments

THE WRITING OF THIS BOOK would have been quite impossible had it not been for the co-operation that I have received from so many persons and institutions, and I record my appreciation to the following.

To the New Zealand Railways Department a very large debt indeed is owed. Engine passes are given to members of the public only very rarely. Some idea of the co-operation I have received from the Department can be found in the words of one senior official: "Mr Leitch, you have had more engine passes than any other man in the history of the railways." Without the splendid response on the part of the Department this book could never have been more than a daydream in the mind of its author. To the Chief Mechanical Engineer, Mr L. Johnston, and his predecessor, Mr H. Purchase, under whose signatures the passes were issued, and to Mr A. N. Palmer, the Publicity Manager, who approved my many requests and readily gave permission to make use of Departmental historical material, many thanks are due.

I made many friends among the engine crews with whom I travelled, and almost without exception these good fellows cheerfully put up with my presence and inquisitive mind in the cabs of their locomotives. I am indebted to them immensely, and I regret being unable to mention them all by name, but the old Army adage of "no names, no pack drill", is obviously relevant. Several guards in different parts of the country allowed me to travel in their vans and this, too, was much appreciated. I look back with very real pleasure on the hospitality I have received from so many drivers, firemen, and guards in the course of my travels.

Considerable help has been accorded by the staff of the Alexander Turnbull Library and from Miss V. Watson of the Masterton Public Library, in tracking down many unusual source materials for the more academic research that has gone into the preparation of this book. Mr T. C. Pant, Joint Director of the

Research Institute of the Indian Railways, kindly read the material on "The Great Motive Power Debate" and the comments of this expert in the field have been of considerable benefit to this book.

Mr Pat McKeown, the Masterton Chief Stationmaster, frequently rang depots and stations all over the country assisting me to plan trips; Mrs Cora Pinder reduced my handwritten hieroglyphics to neat typescript; Mr G. E. A. Nikolaison of Masterton, and Mr R. Hazelwood of the *Wairarapa Times-Age* have been of great assistance on the photographic side. My thanks go to all of them.

Lastly I thank my wife, who spent two wedding anniversaries and many hours by herself while her husband was hundreds of miles away riding railway engines, who sat through many evenings while an oblivious spouse sank himself in writing, and who has encouraged me throughout.

D.B.L.

Introduction

FOR A SURPRISINGLY LARGE NUMBER of people in all walks of life, railways hold a great fascination. Most people will spare more than a passing glance at a train moving through the countryside, particularly if a snorting, smoke-billowing, steam engine happens to be on the head end.

From my earliest, terrified, small-boy memories of a K or Ka bearing down on Feilding station with all stops out while I clung trembling to my mother's skirts, the magnificent might and thundering power of the steam locomotive have been for me an enduring fascination.

The steam engine has occupied a unique position for over 130 years. A mere piece of steam-actuated machinery bound to steel rails, a mere means of transportation; yet no other object with the possible exception of the sailing ship has ever captured the minds and imagination of so many people, nor been endowed with so many animate and human qualities. It has been the means to Empire, to trade, development, prosperity. Its lonely whistle echoing down the night has inspired poets and dreamers, and kindled in many the unquenchable wanderlust that cannot hear a train whistle without an itching in the feet.

The railways and steam locomotives of New Zealand take second place to none in interest, as a perusal of any overseas book on railways will prove, with its usually extensive section on the Dominion's trackage and equipment. It has been my great fortune to have seen so much of the New Zealand railways system from that most interesting viewpoint of all – the footplate.

It is with such travels, on diesel and electric engines as well as on steam, that this book is largely concerned. It is, I hope, a book to be read with enjoyment, rather than to be learned and inwardly digested. The reader will not find in these pages details of the number of rivets on the tender of a Ka, nor the date upon which every little section of track was laid. I hope that, instead, the reader will join me for a pleasant amble over a number of lines, both sleepy branch and busy main, and for a very few serious discussions and a large number of pleasant and at times nostalgic looks at, and trips on, the locomotives and trains of the New Zealand railways.

Masterton   D.B.L.

1

Express steam

AILWAY JOURNEYS VARY GREATLY according to the individual tastes of the passenger. For many, the thought of a railway trip undoubtedly conjures up visions of the rush for a soggy pie and cup of black tea at Taihape on a cold winter's night during one of the refreshment stops on the long Main Trunk trip. It may perhaps conjure up memories of more pleasant trips at a faster pace over a shorter distance in the relative comfort of a railcar. But for the enthusiast, any trip is a small adventure in itself, and in most cases more so if the motive power is steam. To sit in a carriage while a Ka panted its way up the spiral or sped over the Shannon straights was a sensation of sheer delight, as the whistle howled for country crossings and the couplings clashed and banged all through the long night.

Any express trip is exciting; it offers smells, the noises, the speed, or the slow laboured grind up a bank but these are as nothing compared with the sheer exuberant excitement of an express trip from the footplate. I was extremely fortunate in obtaining permission to make my first footplate run—to Taihape, at the head of Train 626, the Wellington-Auckland Express, in the last days of passenger steam haulage on the Main Trunk. The trip was one of the greatest railway experiences that anyone could ever expect to have.

On a fine sunny summer afternoon in late January 1965 I arrived at the Paekakariki locomotive depot armed with a pass, camera, and notebook, and introduced myself to the foreman. He glanced at the looming bulk of Ka957 standing simmering in the warm sunshine.

"Ever been on one of these before?" he asked, looking at me quizzically.

I had to confess that at that stage I hadn't.

"Hmmm," he frowned. "Well for Pete's sake hang on!"

To me in my then state of relative innocence, this was an odd remark. The engine looked peaceful enough, quietly simmering and from time to time releasing a small stream of water from her valve chests with an apologetic *pop*. What could be less disturbing?

I met my crew, Maurie the driver and his fireman, John, and again came the question: "Ever been on one of these before?" The foreman grinned and shouted something about "give him a thrill", to the crew. I was to get that all right, on one of the most wildly exciting rides that in my opinion it is possible to experience — the awful sensation of a Ka at speed.

The trip started quietly enough. At about 4.20 p.m. a klaxon blared and 626, under the charge of one of the superb Ew class electrics, glided smoothly into the Paekakariki Station. Aboard 957 on the loop, Maurie let out the reverse lever and eased back on the regulator and we chuffed quietly down the loop to hook on to the 12-total train. I was standing humbly and unobtrusively out of the way, back by the tender, with one foot on the tender deck and the other on the connecting plate over the engine-tender coupling.

I was somewhat shocked to have the fireman suddenly yell: "Hey, don't stand there!"

In my blissful ignorance, I had one foot just behind the lip of the connecting plate. The plate, had it moved, could have sliced off the bottom of my foot as we crossed over to the main. The plate is filed razor-sharp by the constant friction as it moves about with the movements of the locomotive. At another time, a driver was to tell me that he'd had the bottom completely cut off a thick steel toolbox when he had inadvertently forgotten to shift it before getting under way. I glanced around with new respect and altered my position accordingly.

Soon, 957 had been coupled on to the train. The guard's whistle shrilled, the green flag waved, the driver blew a long blast on the whistle, eased off the brakes and gently opened the regulator. With a mighty puff from the stack the great coupling-rods moved, the huge driving-wheels slowly began to turn, and with another whistle blast to acknowledge "Guard aboard", we were off on the first stage of our run to Taihape.

As the cut-off lever was brought back and the regulator opened out, the big engine steadily increased speed on the long straight to McKay's Crossing. Although we were not travelling at speed as yet, the engine was becoming very unstable underfoot to one then unused to it, and it was good to subside on to the extended portion of the fireman's seat that I was offered — with a grin. It was just as well that I sat down, because as we rounded the curve north of the crossing the regulator was opened out and the cab filled with the staccato roar of the Ka's exhaust as we swept along beside the main highway, the Ka almost disdainfully racing past the cars that were vainly trying to keep up with us.

With the speed came unbelievable exhilaration as 145 tons of locomotive and 400 tons of carriages hurtled over the plains to Levin. The big engine was literally galloping by this time, as the force of the pistons whipped the wheels around, almost lifting them from the track. John and Maurie were gently moving up and down in time to the rhythm and by following suit I gained an immediate relief to the bouncing that threatened to loosen my teeth. The "Iron Horse" is no misnomer! Again and again as we hurtled into a bend it seemed impossible that we would not simply charge straight off into the side of a cutting. The length of the great boiler rocked and swayed, and at the last minute, as we seemed headed for certain destruction, it jolted and followed the tracks around.

John leaned across to Maurie and shouted some unintelligible remark about sand, to which Maurie nodded in reply. The fireman, balancing easily, moved to the tender and took a dipperful of white sand from a box on the front of the tender. He knocked aside the firebox cover and sprinkled the sand into the firebox. The exhaust, which had, to say the least of it, been noticeable, increased to an earshattering, clattering, roar as the sand blasted through the tubes, clearing them of soot and oil sludge and giving better steaming. Great gouts of black smoke shot upwards and blotted out the sun for a few minutes until the sand had been exhausted.

Then came the surprise. The fireman turned on a tap and proceeded to hose the floor of the cab until it was shining-clean, and all the particles of sand had been washed away. I found that a small handbrush was standard equipment in every fireman's bag and I was surprised at the frequent use that was made of it. It seemed in such complete contrast to the grease and grime on the outside of the boiler.

Soon we were coasting into Levin and while we paused there Maurie moved around the engine, checking the moving parts. Soon we were off again on the fastest part of the trip, over the Makerua Plains. The sense of awful power that a Ka at speed instils into the footplate initiate practically beggars description. The tender-plates clatter and bang, the windows rattle in their frames, the exhaust bellows, steam hisses, the whole engine rocks

B

and sways alarmingly, and careers along at an almost frightening speed.

As we raced on in the sunlight of that late summer afternoon it was impossible not to recall the earlier speedsters whose driving wheels had churned through this same stretch of countryside. The great Baldwin-built locomotives of the old Wellington and Manawatu Railway Company, whose name never fails to evoke vistas of clerestory roofs, tolling brass bells, and Yankee dash. It was of course along this same stretch of track that the W & M Ry Co had established a then world record for narrow gauge steam with a speed of 64·4 mph in 1892. A speed, let it be noted, that modern diesels would have to be well notched up to attain.

One driver friend of mine once swore to me that he had been firing a Ka (he thought 954) on the Limited when a speed of 75 mph was attained in an effort to make up time. Allowing for unreliable speedometers and the natural blurring of memory, the speed nevertheless must have been quite exceptional. Given a good crew, a clean boiler and a good track, there is nothing technically impossible in a Ka reaching such a speed.

By this time, we ourselves were forging along at almost 60 mph and to me it seemed like the "ton". Steam engines are deceptive machines: the easily seen and heard power acts on the imagination, and it took me several trips to guess with any degree of accuracy the engine's speed without reference to such obvious aids as mileposts. Before this I would be as much as 15 mph out with my guess — all on the excess side of the line.

From time to time the driver checked the Detroit lubricator which maintains an even flow of lubricating oil to the pistons. The fireman was keeping an eye on his steam pressure gauge and working the injector as the boiler water-level dropped. As we pounded on, the tablet was placed in the bracket on the side of the cab and exchanged with a crash at little country stations for the token which gave us the right to roar on into the next section of track without pause. On the flat easy run to Palmerston North, while always busy, the work is light compared to that which the fireman faces on the graded sections of the line. Both men kept a wary eye on the signals, and the cry "Green up!" ensured no slackening of speed.

At Shannon, John and Maurie exchanged trains with the crew of a southbound Da powered goods, and with a blast of the whistle we were steaming noisily away again. Around Linton the ride was appallingly rough over old track, and the noise was such that I could talk to the fireman only by shouting directly into his ear —

and even then half of my questions and most of his replies were lost amid the infernal noise that was like a thousand high-pitched pneumatic drills in our ears.

Soon we were flashing past the Longburn Freezing Works and on to the Milson Deviation as the old City line (now being ripped up) turned off to the Palmerston North loco sheds.

At the time of this trip Palmerston North was still very much in the steam locomotive business and the new line was still known as "the Deviation". Palmerston's smart new station glided past as the brakes hissed on and I met my new crew, Fireman Colin and his driver mate Jim. While the passengers slaked their thirst in the buffet, 957 was uncoupled and run down to the water tank to guzzle some 2,500 gallons of water. She had certainly earned her drink. The small and not-so-small boys who are a feature of every stop gazed with decided envy at the obviously amateur railwayman clambering possessively over the tender of 957, but by now I was feeling part of the crew and felt obliged to act accordingly!

Soon the urgent clang of the station bell announced that it was time to be on our way again. We swept out of the yards and on to the main in a roar of sound and fury, Colin asking Jim when he could sand, and busily explaining the intricate dials and wheels to me. On the long straight from Bunnythorpe to Feilding the regulator was opened out and the sand again poured into the fire-box as the smoke pall drifted over the green fields of the Manawatu and the long train rocked and swayed as it beat its way northwards.

We whistled our way out of Feilding as twilight was approaching, and the sun was setting in a brilliant haze of orange and red as we rocked our way up the Halcombe hill and on towards Marton. The countryside was beginning to include more cuttings, and banks and curves were becoming more frequent. The big Ka still bellowed wrathfully and maintained her speed, but already the fireman was noticeably busier than his predecessors had been on the early stages. With a satisfying welter of sound we took the Kakariki Bank and the big engine faltered temporarily as the 400 tons behind dragged at her drawbar. We rolled into Marton as the last golden glow of a sunset played on the boiler and the racing shadow alongside perceptibly lengthened.

At Marton, 957 thirstily took on more water for the steam-consuming run that was ahead of her. Steaming freely and raring to go, she pulled out of Marton and headed off into the twilight-shadowed Rangitikei country. The great white cliffs of the Rangitikei River had never seemed so beautiful to me as they did that fine summer evening viewed from a Ka climbing steadily into the hill country, her exhaust somehow peaceful in the calm still air as her smoke drifted up into the darkening sky. Man, machine, and Nature were one in a picture of natural and mechanical beauty that will never be seen again.

Night fell. The great yellow headlight of the Ka swept over the cuttings and across the valleys as the wheels of the big engine pounded around the curves and up the grades on the Mangaweka approaches. Now we were climbing in earnest and the deafening bark of the exhaust increased in pitch as the smoke belched from the stack into the clear night air. With a reverberating roar we crossed the mighty spans of the Makohine and Mangaweka viaducts, just two of the massive spans that engineers of the past had been forced to design and build in order that the country might enjoy the blessings of a railway. At 6 mph we crawled along past a tremendous slip near Mangaweka where a whole hillside was on the move and 24-hour watches were being kept. We accelerated away into the night again. The light from the firebox flickered and glowed and its reflections danced on the surrounding hillside.

The fireman was now constantly on the move, working injectors, checking the boiler water-level, operating the draught to ensure that the hard working engine lacked no assistance in her efforts to move her train up the grade. The driver was peering ahead, watching for the first of several tunnels that would shortly be approaching.

A shriek of the whistle heralded a sudden plunge into the very bowels of the mountain. Smoke blasted up against the roof of the tunnel while the light of the fire was dimmed as stifling, pungent smoke drifted into the cab. My eyes watered and the air sucked into my lungs was hot and tasted of gritty oil fumes. Suddenly, when the heat and smoke were becoming almost unbearable, we burst out into the night air and gratefully sucked clean air into our burning lungs. Most of the remaining tunnels were on a downgrade, and with the drifter working the smoke was no problem, but the heat was still uncomfortable and the night air was like a brief cold shower as we emerged into the open again.

The whistle echoed around the hillsides as we flashed over dusty country-road level crossings, and hurtled through little whistle stops along the line. Like a great undersea monster with luminous eyes the rest of the train snaked along behind, carriage windows shining brightly. In the cars, on soft reclining seats, the passengers read and dozed, in cosy contrast to the shattering roar, the whistling wind, the clatter of the swaying locomotive cab – and I wouldn't have changed places for anything.

Soon the lights of Taihape loomed up out of the valley as we wheeled out of a cutting. The exhaust was shut off while we drifted into the station and coasted gently to a halt. While the platform echoed to the hustle of feet as passengers surged for the tea rooms, 957 was uncoupled from her train and rumbled off to clear the main. Her relief backed on, and train 626 was ready to roll again.

With her job well done, 957 trundled down to the turntable, was turned and driven slowly down to the sheds. The tender supplies of fuel and water were replenished after the consuming run from Marton, and fresh sand was placed in the box on the tender. The crew moved around with big compressed-air grease-guns, greasing and checking the moving parts. The fire was notched down and the big loco allowed to sit in the shed, simmering and popping like a giant coffee percolator, until with the arrival of the southbound express it would be time for her to hitch on her train and roll southwards.

But now, the Ka's roar has gone for ever from the Makerua Plains, the Mangaweka Valley and the North Island ranges, for the romance of steam has faded before the cold reality of the grumbling diesel. Its epitaph is the sound of a mobile generating plant and the soulless bleat of a klaxon where once steam, in all its awesome majesty, was supreme. Those of us who have stood bathed in the orange glow of a fire on a swaying footplate, or thrilled from a hillside as a steamer howled her defiance at a grade, can do no more than stand and mourn.

The fireboxes have gone cold. The life has departed for ever from the proud Kas: the aristocrats of New Zealand steam.

2

Driving and firing

THERE WAS A TIME when it was the ambition of most small boys to be an engine driver, to emulate that godlike figure in the peaked cap (and, in days gone by, a black shirt and spotless white tie) who drove the great black engine at the head of the train, and who could make or break the day by waving or not as he roared past at what seemed incredible speed. In these days of more complex marvels of jets and rockets, the ambition seems less frequently expressed, but there are doubtless many grown men in whom such desire once smouldered. Most dreams tend to suffer somewhat once the reality is experienced; but the tremendous sense of power and awe that comes from handling the controls of a steam locomotive for the first time is not easily forgotten. Such has been my privilege, and a fascinating experience it was.

Before the engine is ready to be driven however, there are a multitude of tasks to be carried out. For the regular crew, the duties involved in preparing, running, and putting away an engine – steam, diesel or electric – are routine, and simply a part of the important and vital job that they have to do. To anyone who is not a railwayman it is a fascinating, complicated, and at times a mysterious, collection of functions and actions that culminates in the workings of a main line train. I have been lucky enough to have been allowed to drive and fire both oilburning and coalburning steam locomotives, as well as to observe at first hand the duties of electric and diesel crews.

My first introduction to the inner mysteries of locomotive running was at Palmerston North. I held a pass for travel on the footplate of the engine hauling train C33, a weekend passenger train to Wellington and a remote survival of the famous old "Field's Express", unofficially named for the man who fought so hard for its introduction. Waiting on shed for her crew was Ka931, quietly simmering as she basked in warm sunshine outside the decrepit

sheds of the old locomotive depot. She was on the way to full
working pressure, having been already prepared to a large extent
by the shed crew, from whom the road crew take over the engine.

While the fireman deposited his bucket containing cotton waste,
broom, lunch-tin and other essential items of equipment, and
proceeded to notch up the oilfed fire, the driver made a long and
extensive survey of the running gear. All bearings, rods, links,
and wheels came under his critical eye. The odd spot of grease
was applied where he thought the shed crew had been lax, and then
the engine was eased over the inspection pit to check the brake
gear.

It was a curious sensation sitting in a pit with 145 tons of
locomotive standing a few inches above me. All sorts of interesting
possibilities, like someone knocking the drain cock in the cab off
and showering us with boiling water, or the grate suddenly falling
out or the wheel spokes (which from the outside looked so strong
and from down here so thin) collapsing, occurred to me as I
crouched beneath the so obviously alive monster. It was probably
a special form of claustrophobia and it was not without relief that
I crawled back out and saw 931 from the proper perspective again.

The fireman meantime had been busy checking that the oil and
water were "all systems go", cleaning the cab windows and the
gauge glasses, and checking that there was a good supply of tube
sand in the box on the tender. Some 45 minutes after signing on,
the crew and their engine were ready for the road. It had taken
much more than this however to get 931 ready for her trip to
Paekakariki. She had not been used the previous day, and required
lighting up from cold.

In an oilburner, this is a greatly differing process from that
used in steaming up a coalburning locomotive. In any steaming
up process, the first essential is to get enough steam raised to
enable one to operate the various controls, one of the more
important at this stage being the blower, which creates the draught
for the fire to burn more fiercely, as well as such essentials as the
brakes. On an oilburner, there is an almost vicious circle in that
the burner which sprays the oil into the firebox, uses steam; if
there's no steam there's no oil, and therefore no fire. If there's no
fire then how can there be any steam?

This apparent dilemma is solved in two ways, one easy, and the
other long and tedious. In the easy method, an "in-steam" engine
is run alongside and a steam hose connected to a special fitting in
the cab of the dead engine. In this manner steam is piped into the
dead locomotive until there is sufficient to operate the burner. At

this juncture an oily rag is lit, tossed into the firebox and the burner turned on. There is a hollow crump and presto! – one has hungry flames licking around the firebox. From then on it is simply a question of keeping up the oil flow, until after a period of up to two hours, the engine has a full head of steam. While in an emergency steam can be, and on occasions such as an engine failure on an express, has been, raised in considerably shorter time than this, the uneven rate of expansion of various parts in the boiler and tubes can do serious damage to an engine if persisted in. When an engine has been used the previous day she may still retain sufficient pressure to operate the controls, in which case the burning rag and perhaps one or one and a half hours will see her on the road.

The other method mentioned is much more difficult and time-consuming, and that is raising steam with a wood fire. Fortunately this is fairly rare as most larger depots have another engine in steam or a stationary boiler which may be used. The wood process is long and tedious. The front must be taken off the fire-box in order to allow the wood to be placed in the firebox. Oil-burners do not have the customary fire door, only what is in effect a peephole, through which the sand for tube scouring is poured. Using the wood method usually takes up to four hours before the locomotive is ready for the road.

At about half past three, Ka931 was ready to move out and run around to the new Palmerston North Station. At that time, this involved something like eight miles of light running, and the waste of time can readily be appreciated. It was a far cheaper practice for the engine crews, more particularly of diesels, to leave their engines in the main yards and be collected by car to be run across town to sign off, than have them bring their engines into the town depot. We left the depot in company with a Da on a push-me-pull-you basis, but at Milson we parted company, the Da to head a freight drag up the trunk, and ourselves to hook on to the eight total "express" waiting at the No 1 Platform, a combination of old wooden cars and the prewar steel-panelled vehicles.

It was a beautiful summer afternoon, and the trip was obviously going to be a pleasant one. With a train of only 209 tons total, timekeeping was no problem except that frequent checks had to be made to ensure that we were not running ahead of time on the very generous timetable allowed. The trip was leisurely and speeds rarely exceeded 45 mph, even on the best stretches of the line.

For all her 25 years, 931 was running extremely freely and was a most comfortable riding engine.

It was at Waikanae that the driver gave me the chance of a lifetime. "Would you like to have a try?"

He had obviously noticed my careful survey of his movements with the controls and I was nothing if not eager – Opportunity may only knock once!

"Reckon you know what to do?" he asked.

I gave a quick résumé of my intended actions.

"Sounds fair enough," he commented. "Sit down, and I'll keep a tight eye on things."

I sat down, I was in the driver's seat of a Ka, one of the most powerful locomotives on the New Zealand Railways, and in a few moments it would be my hands and brain that would be directing the movements of the huge body of machinery. I might add, however, that the driver was right beside me, ready in an instant if I looked like doing the wrong thing. The backhead loomed before me, a maze of pipes, levers, and gauges, all having their own unique function in the workings of this animate giant.

Despite their apparent complexity, however, the controls of a steam locomotive are not difficult to manipulate, so as to cause the locomotive to move. But the skill that is acquired only through years of experience is in the delicate manipulation of the controls to obtain the best possible performance with the least waste of steam and wear on the engine. This is something that no amateur can ever acquire. I could and did drive the engine, as did the driver; but I can paint a picture and so could Rembrandt and Da Vinci! Therein lies the comparison.

The driver of a steam locomotive has several controls, of which the two most important are the regulator and the reverse lever. The regulator, as its name implies, regulates the supply of steam to the cylinders, while the reverse, or cut-off lever, determines the position in the piston stroke at which the steam is cut off. When the steam is cut off, the steam already in the cylinders completes its work by natural expansion. When starting, the cut-off is well advanced, it may be almost at maximum, which means that for most of the piston stroke the motion is carried out by steam being admitted for almost all the stroke without using any of its expansive properties. As the train gets under way, it needs less power and the cut-off is brought back until at, say, 15 per cent cut-off, steam is being admitted to the cylinders for only about one-seventh of the stroke and is doing the rest of the work by expansion.

For flat fast running, the regulator will be well out, giving a greater amount of steam in the cylinders, but conserving it by admitting it for only the small time fraction needed. Conversely, as the engine strikes a grade, the cut-off is reduced, so that the greater quantity of steam (open regulator) is applied in the cylinders for longer periods, and thus gives the greater power required for the heavier work. The skilled driver regulates both controls constantly as the nature of the road, and therefore the demands on the engine, constantly change. A subsidiary control is the drifter, which is used on downgrades, when momentum rather than steam is doing most of the work. This lever admits a small amount of steam to the cylinders, enough to keep the pistons "lubricated" without actually driving them.

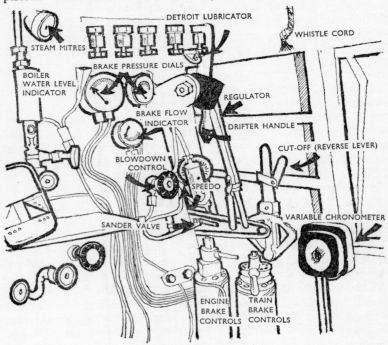

Main driver's controls on a Ka locomotive.

Besides these, however, the driver has other controls for differing purposes. Sanding gear is essential when the engine needs extra friction on the wheels for starting, or on difficult grades, and in particular when the tracks are greasy or wet. The small sanding valve controls the admission of dry steam into an ejector, which draws sand from the dome on top of the boiler, down lead pipes, and sprays it in front of the first and third (on a Ka) driving wheels.

Important items of equipment also are of course the brakes. Fortunately the old days when the only way to stop a train was to slam the reversing lever over into reverse and hang on while the wheels spun and slipped, have long gone, and Westinghouse brakes are standard equipment on all trains. Most modern locomotives have a train brake and an engine brake mounted on pedestals near the driver's waist. In normal running the train brake, which is easier acting, is used; the engine brake is more direct and is used, in most cases, only as an emergency brake complementary to the train brake.

In addition, the driver must keep an eye on the air and brake pressure gauges, and the brake flow indicator, all of which tell him whether the braking system is working properly or not. Any leak in the brake pipes will immediately register on the brake flow indicator, warning that part of the braking system has failed.

An important item of equipment is the Detroit hydrostatic lubricator. While lubrication can easily be applied manually when the engine is at rest to some parts where only intermittent attention is required, on other parts where constant lubrication is needed different methods apply. Siphons or pads may be used for axlebox lubrication, but for many of the motion details, the crossheads slide-valve, etc., as well as the cylinders, hydrostatic lubrication is generally used. In this type of lubricator, used on the New Zealand Railways, steam condenses and the resulting water displaces an equivalent amount of oil. The drops of oil rise in a glass tube filled with water which makes it a simple matter to check and adjust the feed by the feed-regulating valves at the bottom of the lubricator.

The one remaining major item of equipment is the blowdown. This fitting revolutionised modern steam practice, and appreciably lengthened the intervals between boiler cleans. Engines with this type of fitting require on the average a manual clean-out every 28 days, as opposed to every 10 or 14 days. Certain carefully-measured chemical agents are automatically introduced into the feed water, and have the effect of preventing the deposit of scale on the heating surfaces. The chemical ingredients help reduce the scale to sludge, which collects at the bottom of the boiler and is periodically flushed out with steam by the application of the blow-down valve.

These then, were the variety of controls ranged in different positions in front of me. It was now over to me to get the train rolling. I glanced back down the train to where the guard stood waiting for the last passenger to get on. Suddenly, there it was, the green flag!

I reached up for the whistle cord and tugged, and the blast of a Ka's whistle sliced through the shimmering air. Brakes hissed off as I pulled the shiny brass lever. I advanced the cut-off a few notches and pulled gently back on the regulator and the steam hissed into the cylinders. The great wheels were moving slowly round as I glanced back, saw the guard step on to the van and wave again. Another whistle blast signalled "guard aboard" and it was time to open her out another few notches, and pull back the cut-off lever a little further. The pistons slid back and forth ever faster as the old Ka got the bit between her teeth and settled down into a steadily increasing pace. We blasted over a crossing and rattled along by the main highway as I progressively gave her her head with a careful interplay of the cut-off and regulator. When the speedo needle flickered on the 50 reading I held her steady, and only then came the realisation that this really was me driving this hurtling projectile. It was time to come down to earth.

"Nice going, Casey, but you'd better let me have her now, there's a speed restriction coming up shortly," grinned the driver. I slid out of the driver's seat and turned the regulator over to him. It had been a tremendous experience. A great piece of steel weighing 145 tons, exercising over 32,000 lb of tractive effort, and moving down two slim rails at 50 mph had been mine to command. No lord in his castle or general with his army ever felt such a sense of power and achievement — or such deep respect for the men who had designed, built, driven and maintained such a magnificent example of steam engineering.

My second experience of "eye on road and throttle in hand" was on an Ab, No 823, on the Wild West Coast. I was footplating on the daily Greymouth-Ross and return mixed train when the opportunity arose. We had arrived at Ross shortly before lunch, and after we'd watered the engine it was time to think about getting her turned for the trip home. The straight side of the wye at Ross runs through the engine shed in which stood Ab722, cold and lifeless. The shed had to be opened up, and we reversed in and bumped gently into the back of 722 and pushed her off down to the end of the track.

The wye, or turning triangle, at Ross must surely be one of the most picturesque engine turning devices in the country. No turntable here with lumps of coal and dirt in the bottom of the pit, no wye sitting desolate out in the middle of a paddock. The Ross wye runs through a beautiful little stand of native bush which was green and glistening in hot sunshine. The soft chuffing of the Ab mingled with bird calls as she rolled down one side of the triangle through the ferns, creepers, and trees of the glade. The reverse lever swung over, she rolled back down the other side, once more through the engine shed, and towed back into its dim shadow 722, to resume her interrupted slumbers.

It was over lunch that I questioned the driver on the techniques of Ab driving, and mentioned that this was for comparison with a Ka.

"Hell," was his rejoinder. "Why waste our lunchtime talking about it? You take her back up to Hokitika, that's better than me trying to tell you with a mouthful of sandwich!"

So it was that we whistled out of Ross; with the driver insisting that he would do the firing and his mate could double as the enthusiast for a few miles. The Ab was different from Ka931, in that on these older engines the levers are worked by muscle power alone. The J and K classes have power-assisted reverse levers which move easily to the desired notch. The Abs' Armstrong patent is a different kettle of fish altogether. 823 had a fairly stiff lever and to start off I had to plant one foot on the backhead and heave bodily to shift the brute. The regulator is mounted horizontally to the boiler backhead and until one gets used to this, it is harder to gauge the setting than on a Ka, where the lever hangs vertically from the side of the backhead.

We moved off and with a short train were soon rattling merrily along at a regulation 30 mph through the bush and swamp characteristic of this section of the line. All too soon for me, we arrived at the Hokitika bridge. We must have made good time because we arrived a few minutes early and had to wait for a signal change before crossing the bridge. The line from Ross to Hokitika is "open section" on which trains may not arrive early at Hokitika, but may run within the section fairly freely as they please. As we crossed the old bridge it was time to vacate the right-hand seat. As if at the wave of a magic wand everyone changed places and duties, and I was once again the observer.

In marked contrast to the maze of controls that adorn the

steam engine cab, is the spartan set-up of the diesel locomotive.
A bank of dials and switches sits at the driver's left hand, while in
addition he has the throttle lever, reverse lever, dynamic brake
control, air-brake handle, sander, deadman's pedal (which causes
the brakes to be automatically applied unless it is kept depressed),
light switches, horn cord, ammeter which indicates the load on
the generator, the air-flow indicator, and finally the cab heater
and windscreen-wiper switches. It is simple, orderly and compact,
and without doubt more convenient for the driver.

The diesel driver sits all the time he is driving, unlike the steam
engine driver who must check his lubricator from time to time
and may have to stand to gain leverage with a non-powered
reverse or to attend to any other of several controls and indicators
which may require his attention. The most important lever, the
throttle, controls the governor on the diesel engine, and accelerates
it through a range of speeds from idling to top, taking it up by
progressive steps of some 75 rpm on the average, from an idling
speed of about 270 rpm to something like 850 rpm. It takes but
a short time to master the principles of diesel driving, and the
average period of practical instruction to turn a certified steam
driver into a diesel ticket man is only seven days.

No less important than the driver, however, at least on a steam
locomotive footplate, is the fireman. After all, the driver can pull
his regulator all day but he'll get precisely nowhere if there's no
steam in the boiler. Firing on a coalburning steam engine calls for
strong arms and a good brain, and either without the other will
never result in a good fireman. Shovelling coal for hours on end
requires strong arms, but unless the fireman watches his fire,
injects the water at the right time, and knows the road, he'll never
make the grade. The art of building a good fire from which the
best steaming will be obtained is a precise one. With a long narrow
firebox, as on the B class engines, the coal must be thrown well
forward, whereas with the wider firebox of the Ab or J, the sides
require equal attention as the fire must be spread evenly over the
grate surface.

A good fireman is the man who can keep the steam pressure
needle hovering near the maximum without the waste of blowing
off when the pressure is exceeded. To this end he must fire in
anticipation, not of the present demand, but of the demand he
anticipates the engine will make. He will begin firing before a
grade begins, so that there's a full head of steam exactly when the
driving-wheels bite into the slope. Nearing the top of a rise he

ceases firing so that the steam won't rise too far on the downgrade, when less will be required.

It was on a goods train headed by Ab823 again that I found out what it was like to be a fireman. We were plodding steadily along in driving rain south of Inangahua on the Coast when the fireman turned to me.

"Just how much of an enthusiast are you?"

It seemed an odd question, and I wasn't quite sure what to say. "Well, pretty enthusiastic I suppose," was all I could manage, still fairly mystified.

"Right, let's see some of that enthusiasm," he grinned. "Grab the shovel, two left back, two left front, same on the right, one down the centre and one up the back!"

I grabbed the shovel, kicked the firebox door open and set to. There is only one way to fire and that is quickly. Anything less than at top speed and the heat pouring out of the open door will almost literally fry you. The technique is to pivot on the right foot, dig into the coal on the plate, pivot, advance the left foot and swing. It all sounds fine in theory and looks deceptively easy, but that rhythm has to be maintained on a bouncing engine deck and it's nowhere near as easy as it sounds. I was on my way, pivot, dig, pivot, heave, and coal flew everywhere as the engine lurched and the shovel hit the firebox mouth with a dull clang. It was not an auspicious start. Back again, pivot, dig, pivot, heave, and into the hungry fire went several pounds of good Westport coal. And so it went for another nine repeat actions. By the seventh I was clearly not fast enough; the heat felt as though it would sear the skin off my arm, my left leg seemed as though it was in the fire instead of beside it. Finally in went the last shovel load and almost shouting with relief I slammed the door on the raging red inferno within. It was then I noticed a suspicious smell of smouldering cloth in the cab. I still have the singed hole in an old pair of trousers to remind me that my first effort was not fast enough!

I was all set to relax when the fireman gave me a friendly prod: "It also needs water you know."

I hastened to the left side of the backhead, spun the little brass wheel and pulled back the injector lever and heard the rumble of water being forced into the boiler. Ahead was a small grade, and a glance at the pressure gauge told me that the initial effort with the shovel was about to become an encore. Once more unto the breach, dear friends, etc.

This time it was not so bad: somewhat faster, and I gained increasing confidence as I got into the necessary rhythm. Soon

Reefton Yards were looming up and as we rattled into the station 823 popped her safeties with a satisfying welter of steam and sound. It may not have been indicative of economic firing but at least I hadn't run the driver short of steam!

In sharp contrast to all this is the sedentary labour of the steam fireman's diesel counterpart. He has very little to occupy himself with. The Das are fitted with a vigilance device which operates on a time sequence. Every few minutes this device emits a whistle, and if a button is not pushed to cut it off the brakes will automatically be applied. The "fireman" pushes this button. He also watches for and calls signals, but his functions are few and easy in comparison with a steam fireman.

It was in recognition of this that when the diesels appeared in increasing numbers, the designation of certain members of the locomotive running department was changed. In place of the familiar cleaners and firemen emerged the diesel age locomotive trainees and locomotive assistants. Although these names applied officially, tradition dies hard, and on steamers at least, the fireman is never called anything but "the fireman" by the men that run the engines. Early in the changeover, the General Manager was obliged to send a fairly strongly worded letter to the Engineers', Firemen's and Cleaners' Association (as it is still known), concerning the functions of the second diesel crew member!

In reply to your letter, I desire to inform you that I am unaware of the term "observer" being applied when referring to firemen employed on De and Df class locomotives. The term has no official approval and attention is being called to that fact.

The EFC Association had made clear that the task of fireman on a diesel was not one that appealed. I have found on the average that, among firemen, the vote in favour of steam is about two to one. The majority, who prided themselves on being skilled tradesmen, were not happy with being, as one put it, "just a bloody passenger". The trade has certainly been reduced from a highly skilled to an almost completely unskilled occupation, a fact that some American railroads demonstrated when, in the middle of the "featherbedding" crisis, they employed elderly, often illiterate, pensioners to ride in the firemen's seats of diesels to comply with States' legislation. Seven years or so sitting in the left-hand seat pushing a button and calling signals could certainly be fairly soul-destroying for a keen man anxious to make a career in an honourable trade.

Top: The Mighty Ka! Awaiting the arrival of Train 626, the express to Auckland, is Ka957, one of the best of this excellent class. It was on 957 that the author rode to Taihape at the head of Train 626.

Bottom: Oozing steam is Ka931 which the author drove on a holiday relief express. She waits for her crew to join her for the run round to Milson station. The Kas, for over twenty-five years, were the glamour engines of the Main Trunk Line.

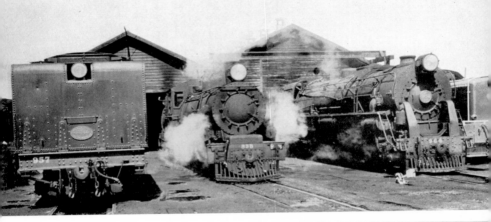

Top: Ka935 enjoys the sunshine beside the water-vat at the old Palmerston North city yards. Once a thriving hive of activity, the depot has vanished like the steam engines it once cared for.

Centre: The air is filled with the hiss of steam, the thump of airbrake pumps and the reek of smoke as Palmerston North depot, in happier days, prepares engines for another day's activity. Pictured are Ka957, Ab838, Ka964, and Dsc444.

Bottom: Sunlight dances on the gleaming boiler of Ab823 as she backs through the bush on the beautiful weed-covered turning-triangle at Ross on the West Coast. The old engine-shed basks in the background.

The life of a fireman on an oilburning locomotive is almost mid-way between the two extremes just mentioned. He doesn't have the heavy work of shovelling coal, but he's still a man with a skilled job to do, as I found on a Ka on the Hawke's Bay Line. We were returning from Takapau to Palmerston North at the time, on Ka933 at the head of a goods, in the early hours of a frosty morn-ing. As we left Matamau, the fireman got up from his seat and beckoned me over from where I had been standing behind the driver.

"Righto Dave, it's time you began to earn your keep. Sit down, she's all yours," he said, pointing to his seat.

Fortunately for the steam pressure in 933, he stood behind me at first and told me what to do until I began to get the hang of things. After that I was on my own, with my fireman friend keep-ing as it were, a foreman's eye on me. As we had a full head of steam and the grade was largely in our favour, the steam pressure had to be reduced before she howled off. The easiest way of reducing is to use the live steam injector, which drains steam from the boiler to inject the water. I pulled the lever, situated near my left knee, towards me, and turned the wheel that opens the steam valve. Keeping a wary eye on the water-level indicator to see that I did not put too much water in, and at the same time watching the steam gauge to see that she didn't fall too low on pressure, almost drove me crosseyed until I shut off the steam and closed the water flow lever.

It was quite an experience to be sitting there, knowing that to all intents and purposes it was now over to me to make sure 933 got the steam she needed to keep her train in motion. Soon it was time to increase the oil flow as we approached a grade. As the driver pulled back on the regulator I eased the oil flow lever around to about the halfway notch. At the same time it was neces-sary to open up the burner, or atomiser as it is sometimes known, to spread the oil, and therefore the fire, over a wider area of the firebox. In much the same fashion as the driver's interplay with regulator and reverse lever, the fireman manipulates the flow and burner to determine the size and corresponding heat of his fire. The pressure needle rose steadily and hovered near the 200 lb to the square inch reading that divides a good head of steam from the waste of a howl-off.

As we crested the grade I eased back on the oil flow, shut off the burner a few turns, and once again used the live steam injector to keep the pressure down.

C

We swung round the curve into Woodville and clattered over the points on to the loop to coast gently to a halt, ready to shunt off some wagons to be collected by a Wairarapa-bound train. I soon found out that there were not only things in the cab to be watched.

"Too much smoke," yelled the driver.

I hastily shut back the blower a bit to ease the draught through the fire, and the churning black smoke gave way to a lighter texture. If there is too much oil flow when steaming, not all the oil will be burnt, which is not only wasteful but makes for a beautiful mess of clogged tubes. There's no doubt that the fire on an oil-burner is easier to control than that of a coalburner. With the former the fire can be shut right off by the moving of a lever, and restarted instantly when necessary. The other advantage was of course the ease of firing: no burnt trousers on this trip; this was steam firing the easy way!

We whistled out of Woodville and headed for the Manawatu Gorge. By this time I knew that the other essential to watch was the driver, and as he opened the regulator for the slight grade at the entrance to the Gorge the fire was roaring from an increased oil flow. The run through the Gorge is on a downgrade and I notched the fire right down and shut it off completely as we clanked through the two long tunnels in the comfortable absence of clouds of smoke.

There's a steep little grade just off the bridge at the western end of the Gorge and it was here that my apprenticeship would be proven. Just before we hit the grade I swung the oil lever round and opened up the burner. The old Ka rocked and banged as she fought her way up, and just before the crest I was ready with the exhaust steam injector to keep the water-level in the boiler up. The exhaust steam injector draws exhaust steam from the smokebox and consequently does not affect the steam pressure in the boiler, so it's the obvious one to use when steaming on grades or building up rather than reducing pressure.

Luck was really with me, and I shut down the flow without dousing the fire and having to resurge momentarily to relight. This problem had been aggravated by a tendency for the oil lever to slip, which didn't make it any easier to gauge the minimum flow accurately. At 5 a.m. we drew into the vast complex of the Palmerston North freightyards, uncoupled and rumbled over the engine flyover to the locomotive depot, where very reluctantly I handed 933 over to the shed fireman to bed down.

So it was that I served my "apprenticeship" as an engine driver and fireman on the New Zealand Railways, under the watchful eye of the crew member who had so splendidly "made" the footplate trip for me by his generosity and friendliness. I look back on such trips with a very real sense of achievement, of having realised an ambition that few amateurs are lucky enough to satisfy.

But perhaps above all, I look back with great respect for those splendid fellows who day and (mostly) night, rain or shine, handle the locomotives that keep our railways moving.

They are a fine breed of men.

3

Petticoat Junction—NZR style

THE READER MAY WELL BE PARDONED for asking, "What on earth has 'Petticoat Junction' to do with the New Zealand Railways?"

At first sight it would appear, very little at all but, strange as it may seem, New Zealand too has its very own version of Petticoat Junction. Televiewers will need no introduction to Petticoat Junction, and whatever the plots of that series may have lacked, doubtless there were many rail fans who sat glued to their sets in the hope of seeing some shots of the old 1890 vintage former Sierra Railroad No 3 laying down a smokescreen. Petticoat Junction, you may recall, was unique in that the train ran when it wanted to, was a permanent part of the local character, and its line was completely divorced from the control of the rest of the railroad. Now while I concede that there may be other contenders, the only line in New Zealand that I consider is worthy of the comparison is the little Waitara Shunt line in Northern Taranaki.

The Waitara Shunt lives in a world remote from the rest of the New Zealand Railways system of which it is nominally a part. It carries goods only, knows nothing so regimented as a timetable, and almost without exception runs only during the day – and then only on weekdays. And everyone, from the shunter to the station-master and engine driver, talks about "Our Train".

The Waitara Shunt is for me the most fascinating of all New Zealand branch lines. It was not always a mere shunt line; in fact the first railway in Taranaki was the New Plymouth-Waitara railway, which was opened for traffic on 14 October 1875, having been built for $82,000. This was rather modest when compared to Taranaki's originally projected line, which would have run from Mokau to Patea and cost something like $4,200,000 to build. This ambitious scheme was dropped however in favour of the New Plymouth-Waitara line, which was surveyed in 1872. For a few years Waitara was a "main line" terminus. Then in 1877 came the writing on the wall so far as its status was concerned. In that year the line was continued on from what is now Lepperton Junction, down to Inglewood, and two years later on to Stratford. Waitara was now a branch line. Passenger traffic in the form of mixed trains, however, continued to run over the line until 1946, when the line became goods only.

Waitara is a small town of some 4,500 people and the town's basic reason for existence is the large freezing works, which in manner similar to the Colossus of old, actually bestrides one of the town's main streets. It is to the freezing works that the little five-mile-long Waitara Shunt owes its continued existence. The main traffic over the line consists of full stock wagons and empty refrigerator cars in, and empty stock wagons and full refrigerator cars out. In addition, as if by way of variety, the line handles the odd wagon of coal and timber, and guard's van parcels traffic.

My attention was attracted to this unique line when visiting friends in Waitara. We were driving out from New Plymouth when a suspicious plume of smoke on the horizon eventually resolved itself into a fussy little Ab with a diminutive train, coasting lazily through the paddocks. It wasn't long before I found myself at the Waitara Station, where I discovered Ab748 wheezing around the yards bunting stock wagons about. Mindful of the unwritten rules applying to enthusiasts' conduct, I chatted to the stationmaster and asked his permission to take some photographs.

It was a rail fan's prayer come true when he said, "Oh, certainly, and while you're here would you like to go for a ride?"

Shades of Deep South hospitality! Taranaki had them all beat that day!!

"Would you rather ride in the van or on the engine?" he enquired. I might have been visiting royalty, judging by his deferential tone. There was, of course, only one reply to such a gracious question and in no time a genial Maori fireman had offered me his seat, I had met my driver, and Ab748 was panting noisily at the head of a train of wagons destined for Lepperton.

The grade out of Waitara Station is reputedly the steepest in the North Island. As no one seemed to know exactly how steep, I am unable to verify this, but an Ab has a rated load of only 220 tons up to Waitara Road, the first loop "station" on the line, three miles from Waitara. The old Ab certainly gave every indication that the going was tough. The line leaves the station on a grade, and to the accompaniment of spinning drivers and hissing steam we began the steep climb. To make it worse, after an initial straight run, the line climbs a bank on 7-chain radius curves. The

old Ab rocked and shuddered alarmingly as we fought our way up
the hill. The cut-off lever was right in and the regulator wide out
as at about 5 mph we bucked our way along. The sanding gear
was being worked constantly, but still the drivers were slipping
and spinning and the exhaust bellowing as if in agony. As we
passed beneath the bridge which carries the main road over the
track, 748 was bucking and staggering like a wounded animal, but
finally we dragged ourselves off the worst of the grade and the
engine settled down into a more even rhythm as the grade began to
ease.

The line itself is very pleasant. It meanders through the lush
Taranaki pasturelands, the weed-grown tracks blending into the
whole green texture of the countryside. The line undulates gently
like a bush tramway and in many places is built on the slope
rather than through it. At one point near Waitara Road, a toetoe
bush grows out from the bank and if the fireman forgets to pull his
head back he gets a vicious slap from the sharp fronds. Finally, at
the four-mile peg, the line climbs through a cutting and levels out
to run alongside the main line for the half mile to Lepperton.

At Lepperton, the Ab shuffled busily around, dropping off her
wagons and collecting those that had been set out for her by main
line freights that had rattled through during the night, or which
may have been left by an engine working a shunt from New
Plymouth. There are no watering facilities at Waitara, so one of
the first chores was to run the old lady under the hydrant and drop
the hose into her half-empty tank. Life is leisurely on the Shunt,
and after perhaps half an hour, or possibly longer if the Lepperton
station agent or the crew of a main line goods have some gossip
to exchange, the Ab trundles off back to Waitara. Because there
are no turning facilities at either Waitara or Lepperton, out trips
are always pilot first, and the engine reverses back home to
Waitara. Even when running light the speed is very modest despite
the downgrade, as reverse running speed limit is 15 mph on the
Shunt.

On our return to Waitara I happened to mention casually that
I'd run out of film and missed a good shot on the grade. "Well,"
said the driver, "that's easy fixed. Come back this afternoon with
some film, and join us for the afternoon run."

This was certainly most handsome hospitality. In the afternoon
we pottered around the Waitara yard doing miscellaneous shunting.
A line of "reefers" had to be shunted over to the works, some coal
wagons were to be run round to the boilerhouse at the freezing
works, and various stock wagons marshalled into a train. At this

stage the fireman, a different fellow from that on the earlier run, left on some mysterious errand and I found myself in his seat assisting with the shunting. This consisted largely of leaning out the window, with my fingers waggling in the vicinity of my posterior, to indicate to the driver whether to keep reversing or not. A sudden shout came to be interpreted as "Watch out or you'll kill the bloody shunter!" Not strictly NZR practice but then, as I have explained, the whole line is nonconformist.

At this juncture the fireman reappeared, back from his mysterious errand in town. The reason for his absence became obvious when he plonked down in the cab a bag containing a large bottle and some pleasant looking "malt essence" inside it. Today, it turned out, was his last day with the railways, and regulations or not, it was to be fittingly celebrated. The crew hastened to explain that it was not their usual custom to furnish refreshments for themselves or their guests and I likewise hastened to assure them that I was not a locomotive inspector in disguise nor a member of the Alliance.

With our respective *bona fides* thus firmly established, it was time to think about getting the show on the road, and we chuffed down on to the main. The train was a large one, all of 38 total, which not only ranks as a monster on the Shunt, but necessitates a trip being made with only half the train as far as Waitara Road because of the loading restriction on the grade.

Once again the valiant little engine toted her 220 tons up the hill, but this time we left the wagons on the loop at Waitara Road and rolled back down to collect the rest of our train which was duly protestingly hauled up the hill and the whole reconnected. We creaked our way on to Lepperton again and shunted the wagons off as the night outside began to close in around us. There were no wagons to be collected, and after watering the engine we decided unanimously that the time to wet the inner man had also arrived. It was a crazy scene. The ruddy light from the fire reflected on the "jar" sitting on the shelf attached to the boiler, the pumps banged and the engine hissed, and three men sat in the soft glow of the fire quaffing from cracked Railway cups. The Ritz could not have been more pleasant. With the jar swaying on the shelf, we chuffed quietly home in the light of a rising moon, back down the weedy tracks to Petticoat Junction.

I next saw the Waitara Shunt again precisely one year later, Easter 1966, when again I met my driver friend of the year before. This time it was 5 a.m. on a frosty Taranaki morning, and a different Ab, 817 was sitting in the diminutive loco shed being fired up for the day's running. Dense black smoke, unassisted by any forced draught, rolled out of her stack from the wood fire burning in her grate.

Lighting up is always done with wood, as a coal fire, besides being difficult to get started, is too fierce and causes the tubes to sweat and distort. Once the fire had heated the tubes sufficiently and raised a few pounds of steam pressure, it was time to start applying the coal, when the blower could be operated to raise the necessary draught. This can generally be done about half an hour after lighting up. At about 50 lb pressure the brake pumps were started while the steam pressure began to rise a little more rapidly. An Ab generally takes three hours to light up from cold, and about an hour if she has been used the day before and the tubes are still warm. The engine can move on about 20 lb pressure and will work to some extent on as low as 50 lb though only with light loads, naturally.

While the steam was rising, it was time to check the running gear. On the older type of engines, the split brasses on the crank pins must be adjusted. The brasses wear, and consequently must be checked and tightened at regular intervals. The newer locomotives with roller bearings do not have this trouble. A nut holding the link to the piston head had worked loose and had to be tightened, and a new cotter-pin on the main driver needed replacing, but otherwise 817 was ready to roll.

Outside, the sun was rising. It was going to be a beautiful day. The engine was run out of the shed, though the shed is so small that even an Ab pokes out at both ends, so getting the whole engine outside does not require much effort. With the guard's van as our only weight on the drawbar we set off in the brisk morning air for Lepperton. Taranaki's pride and joy, Egmont, gleamed pink as the first rays of the sun glistened on her snowfields. The air was bracing, the paddocks white, the sky blue, and the smoke from the Ab satisfyingly thick and black as we puffed our way along.

On our return to Waitara, the fireman faced the unenviable task of coaling up. Waitara has only two crews and one engine and is very much a do-it-yourself depot. Unfortunately for the fireman there are no coalmen or labourers, and the coal has to be shovelled from an La wagon into the buckets, a laborious, time-consuming chore, and then, with the assistance of the little steam crane, swung up into the bunker. At least it was not a case of shovelling from the wagon directly up into the bunker as often happened in the good old days. I could begin to appreciate this fireman's preference for diesel traction.

No 817 was not as good a steamer as 748 and made even heavier weather of the grade out of Waitara. This however could hardly have been blamed on the locomotive, which was in shocking condition. The grime on 817 was inches thick in places. Her number plate was almost indistinguishable. That even her crew felt a little ashamed of her was clear when it was explained that at one time they had religiously cleaned their engines, but when they were invariably replaced with a dirty one from the New Plymouth loco pool the obvious reaction was "Why bother?" Assuredly, no one does. Ab748 had been almost as disreputable and what with the constantly escaping steam from their leaking valves it seemed a miracle that either of them could still steam at all.

The Waitara Shunt was unique in 1966 in that it was still completely steam powered while most of the rest of the North Island system had gone diesel. Unfortunately for the steam enthusiast this happy state is, alas, no more. The Waitara line at time of writing was due to receive a new Db which arrived towards the end of 1966 to replace the grimy Abs that have served it so well for so long. A steam tradition that began with the little A class engines Fox and Ferret has been terminated, and the unique Shunt has become just another minor branch line.

The days of the Waitara crews were also numbered at the time of my visit. "This is an old man's rest home," one of them told me. But when the diesels came, Waitara crews were to be placed on the New Plymouth roster and become liable for weekend and night-shift work. The glamour of the Dbs' working conditions will doubtless rapidly wear off then. When the Ab went, Waitara lost its engine, a tradition in the town and an old and familiar friend, known to most people and all children in Waitara as *Puffing Billy*. Dieselisation means an engine going out to Waitara in the morning from New Plymouth and returning at night, over 100 miles of light running a week which, to the uninitiated, seems strange economics indeed. To everyone who has lived in Waitara, and known "Our Train" or to those who have been fortunate enough to know this fascinating line intimately, the future is bleak. Like Miss Annette Vance of North Carolina, who mourned the passing of the East Tennessee & Western North Carolina Railroad, we may well say:

> *When she passed, we stood amazed,*
> *We admired her so we stood and gazed.*
> *Her loss we pine, we loved her so . . .*
> *Please send us back our little train.*

4

Branch lines and byways

IN THE EARLY DAYS of railway building and development it was
the ambition of every town worthy of the name to be on the
railway. When horses provided the motive power for road
vehicles such an ambition was frequently realised, because the
railway brought with it the blessings of (comparatively) rapid
transport and so was often the means of opening up a potentially
prosperous district to the outside world. Many such lines arose out
of political or local interests rather than national or economic, and
it frequently happened that when better road transport became
available, their potential for operating losses became hard reality.

Not all branch lines fell into this category, as witness the new
branches opening up the exotic forests in the North Island, but all
too often the little lines could not later be justified and, sometimes
quietly but sometimes in a burst of anger or sentimental emotion
from those living along the line, they vanished from the railway
map.

This chapter deals with just some of the little lines. Some were
intended to be part of trunk railways, some never anything but a
local service. Some are still operating while others are just a slight,
faintly discernible mound, running through a paddock. To deal
adequately with the little lines would require a book in itself and
everyone's favourite branch may not be mentioned here. Those
that are, are representative of all that the branch line to somewhere
or nowhere, ever was or still is.

Anyone who journeyed through the Wairarapa in days past, particularly when the old mail trains handled most of the traffic, will
doubtless remember the diminutive brassbound engine and abbreviated train that hissed importantly on a siding at a small station
with the impressive name of Woodside Junction. It was the little
train of the Greytown branch, a representative example in its
growth and decline of branch lines anywhere in New Zealand.

Greytown in the 1870s was a typical little country town, thriving and prosperous, and keenly interested in the railway that was to be built into the Wairarapa. The announcement in 1872 that the line would follow its present course through Woodside was received with thunderstruck amazement by Greytown's citizens. Thunderstruck they may have been, but dumbstruck they were certainly not. Outraged indigation was rampant, and the first of a multitude of railway deputations from the Wairarapa was organised. It brought little cheer however. The villain in the piece was the Waiohine River which engaged in liquid delinquency whenever heavy rain afforded it the opportunity, and it was not considered safe for bridging at any point lower than Woodside. In March 1877 the last deputation was told that the line would stay where it was intended.

Greytown retired temporarily to lick its wounds, but refreshed and invigorated was back again the following year vociferously arguing for a branch line to the town. The petition expressed alarm over: "The great injury their township will suffer from this isolation by being barred from ... the manifold blessing ... of the railway system."

It was an eloquent plea typical of that of many isolated communities, and on 14 May 1880 the line was opened for traffic. The opening was perhaps indicative of the ultimate future of the line. The *New Zealand Times* correspondent noted that: "It rained without intermission, nobody came by train to inaugurate the opening of the railway, there was no procession, no games, no jollification ... there was not what our pubs hoped most for, a big influx of the tourist element."

As if the doubtful opening were not enough, however, worse was to come in the way of a further blow to the damaged corporate pride of Greytown. In September of the same year the mayor informed the indignant citizens that the railways proposed to work the line with *horses*. The inevitable deputation, the formation polished by practice, was quickly formed and the threat of a stables instead of an engine shed was countered and the line settled down to business. Until November 1880 the line enjoyed the status of the terminus of the Wellington line, but lost this elevated position when the section through to Masterton was opened for traffic.

There are few branch lines which do not seem to be somehow especially rurally pleasant, and Greytown's little railway was no exception. The line left the Greytown yard beside a line of the green oak trees that are such a feature of the railways in the Wairarapa. The line was relatively flat and ran through pleasant fields, all the way to Woodside. The sight of a highly polished Wf emerging from behind the leafy shade of the old oak trees, its boiler gleaming black, white wisps of steam hissing importantly from its cylinders, while the smoke curled lazily through the leaves towards a blue sky, was one that few enthusiasts who knew the line will ever forget. The pace was leisurely, 13 minutes being allowed for the easy three-mile-long section, and leisured pleasantness and dignified progress were the orders of the day. After an almost straight run the line curved around a final row of oak trees which filtered the sun's rays and set dappled patterns dancing over the little train as it chugged its unhurried way towards Woodside.

For the first fifty years of its existence the line saw a steady flow of traffic, but the 1920s were for Greytown, as elsewhere, the Roaring Twenties of motorcars and trucks, and the line began steadily to lose its traffic to the newcomers. The little L class tank engines Nos 207 and 219, which had served the line since the turn of the century, gave way to larger Wf engines, Nos 398 and 400, the latter of which was arranged for one-man operation. Traffic continued to decline, however, until in its final years the line was losing some $12,000 per annum. On 24 December 1953 the last train ran, and Greytown lost the railway link that it had fought for so bitterly so many years before.

Now, the station has gone, and only a bank marks where once it stood. The old track formation, covered in broom, can still be traced as it runs through the paddocks, but it has been bereft of rails these many years now. The goods shed still stands, proudly bearing the word "Greytown" for all who may care to glance as they pass by on the adjacent main road. But its dusty interior has not heard the rumble of rolling wagons for years, and it now serves as a petrol store. One or two firebricks, a pile of ash now solid as concrete, and a rusty brake block or two mark the spot where the little engine shed once stood. On a hot day after rain, when the warm moist air rises from the old ash heap, the smell of the railway still lingers and the old familiar odour of warm ash still assails the nostrils. Like White Cliffs, Seaward Bush, Motuhora, Southbridge, Oxford, Donnelly's Crossing, and the other little branch lines whose names are forgotten spots on railway maps, the Greytown branch has vanished into the great limbo of the lost lines.

The many travellers who today roar along in their cars over Provincial State Highway 56 west from Palmerston North doubtless see nothing to suggest a railway on the landscape. But less than 20 feet from their rubber wheels, steel wheels once clattered and bumped along the New Zealand Railways Foxton line.

Foxton, though one could hardly credit it today, was once an important town on the railway system. A wooden-railed horse-powered tramway had been built to Foxton in 1873 but in 1875 the line was taken over by the Railways Department who the following year changed the wood for steel rails and replaced horse-flesh with iron horses. In the days of the Wellington and Manawatu Railway Foxton was the southern terminus of the Government-owned Taranaki line, the Foxton-Wanganui, or Foxton-New Plymouth Railway, depending on the decade in which one happened to be.

In the days of little coasters and barges the wharf at Foxton was vastly different from the odd crumbling pile which is all that remains today. Foxton was then the port for the Manawatu and had a status accordingly. Near by on the bank of the Manawatu River stood the station building, modest yards, goods shed, and engine house of the railway terminus. As well as the NZR, there was of course the daily train of the Manawatu County's Sanson Tramway, which used to run over the NZR tracks from its terminus and junction with the NZR at Himatangi, down to Foxton.

With the acquisition by the Government in 1908 of the Wellington and Manawatu Railway, some of Foxton's mana was lost, when overnight the Taranaki line became the Wellington-New Plymouth Railway and Foxton began the inevitable decline into the status of a branch line from Longburn. So far as its right of way was concerned, Foxton never really lost its tramway status. Its tracks paralleled the Foxton-Palmerston North road for virtually its whole length and followed the road, curve for curve, most of the way. It was devoid of any grades and there was only the merest suggestion of cuttings, mainly through the sandhills at Foxton itself.

It was one of the few lines in the country where the enthusiast could start off at the terminus in his car at the same time the train left and follow to the end of the line without once losing sight of his prey for more than a minute or two. It was the easiest thing in the world to drive sedately along at 20 mph or so, while less than 10 feet away the churning wheels of a little Bb clacked their way along the weed-grown track and the smoke drifted across one's windscreen. It was a railway photographer's paradise.

Today the entire course of the line can still be traced alongside the road from Foxton to Palmerston North. Bereft of rails, sleepers, and trains, it follows the roadway, and with the exception of a lone station building devoid of nameplates sitting drunkenly in a paddock near Himatangi, the old bed is all that now remains of the Foxton line. The outline of foundations and a flat area of riverbank with the remains of a platform and the signs of a cutting are all that marks the Foxton Station. It too has gone into the great lost world of forgotten branches, and civilisation in its relentless march has moved on in search of fresh prey for the all-devouring demon of "Progress".

Many branch lines have been the subject of dark political intrigues and vociferous political agitation; several were built for no better reason than a political gesture by Parliamentarians towards their electorates, without any real concern at all for economics. Just two blatant examples are the Waiuku and Opunake branch lines. On the former, the original daily service was reduced to bi-weekly running immediately after it had been opened, because of the dearth of freight and passengers.

Most agitation and political wrangling in connection with branch lines was of a localised nature and aroused little interest outside the immediate district, but a line that became a national political football, and over which the occasional political tremor is still felt, was the ill-fated Nelson Railway, possibly the best known short line in the country. The repercussions of its abandonment affect politics in the area even today as a result of the 1960-63 National Government's closure, firstly of the Glenhope section and then of the Blenheim link formation works. Today, Nelson is the only sizeable population centre in New Zealand without a railway and the wound to civic pride is still far from healed.

The first railway in New Zealand, ironically enough, was the horse-powered line of the Dun Mountain Copper Mining Company near Nelson, opened in 1862 and closed finally in 1872. The first Government railway was the Nelson-Foxhill section opened on 31 January 1876, and the original conception, and one that persisted throughout the history of the line, was for a link through to the West Coast, and thence to Canterbury by way of Murchison, Inangahua, Brunner, Otira, and Springfield.

After the failure of the Midland Railway Company, Tadmor was eventually reached by 1908, and in December that year Kiwi, 47 miles from Nelson, first saw the smoke of a locomotive. Almost four years later, in September 1912, the line reached Glenhope, destined to become the effective terminus of the line. The political machinations that had accompanied the progress of the line almost from its inception, were to continue for many years as the rails alternately advanced from and then retreated to, Glenhope.

The mixed trains of the Nelson section afforded a slow measured rate of progress through some delightful countryside. There was an initial grade out of town up the hill to Bishopdale, though the return grade from Stoke to Bishopdale was steeper, at 1 in 35, and frequently the little Wf engines would have to set back, sometimes more than once, to get their trains up. It was not unknown for the passengers to have to get out and push at times! Once this obstacle was passed however the line was reasonably flat and free of curves for several miles and there was little strain put on the Wfs as they trundled down the embankment from Hope and skittered across the Waimea River on towards Brightwater and Spring Grove through the fertile farmlands where hops grew in the paddocks beside the line. Spring Grove still has its railway nameboard, standing now forlorn in a paddock on what used to be the station platform of the little settlement.

Leaving Wakefield, the line continued its general south-westerly direction on along the side of a little ridge dotted with trees until just past the 21-mile peg it passed a belt of oak trees and entered the Foxhill yards, the initial terminus of the line. The little station still remains and the faded black lettering of its name can just be discerned on the peeling orange-painted front and ends of the station, now filled with sacks, rubbish, and occupied only by a white goat. A peeling timetable announces faintly the trains that ran in 1936 and warns that the Government will take no responsibility for the late or non-arrival of trains. It was shortly after leaving Foxhill that the little tank engines began to dig their heels in and attack the long climb up to the Spooner's Range tunnel, to emerge again on a downgrade with a pleasant run beside the highway. After crossing the road two or three times, as if to prove the point that the railway had the right of way, the line settled down and the little engines chuffed along a few feet away from the macadam.

At Motupiko at the 31-mile peg, the line ran north along a terrace above the Motueka River for some five miles but then, as if tiring of the view, turned west and crossed the river on a combined bridge of the classical truss pattern. Today the rails can still be seen at either end of the bridge, but no Wf whistle will ever again howl a warning to motorists. The line then ran on through the narrow, fertile fruit-growing Tadmor valley, the hills rising suddenly on either side – a pleasant run on a warm spring day when the willows glistened green, the wind rustled through the trees, and the steam wafted up to join the fleecy clouds in blobs of white in a blue sky.

Around Kiwi and Tui the line entered country that was beginning to roughen and the crops were left behind as the man-made orderliness retreated before the rough strength of Nature's grasses and hills. The line wound around the valley of the Tadmor River, generally avoiding fairly successfully anything in the way of serious grades.

But the mountains that were to prove the railway's master began to close ranks; ferns and scrub together with cuttings and banks became more prominent until the line was struggling through beech forests and mountains as formidable as any King Country landscape, until after the line had climbed to almost 1,500 feet, it ran down into the valley where Glenhope Station nestled beneath the hills.

Today, Glenhope is easily recognised as a former railway station. The building remains, but as a farmer's storeshed; the ladies' waiting-room is stuffed with bales of hay, the ticket office filled with sacks of super, and the whole edifice still painted light orange with brown trim. Outside there is an old coal pile, mostly dust, one or two rusting brakebeams and blocks, the loading bay, stock pens and two ash and inspection pits over which the Wfs dropped their fires. A bird warbles up in the bush, but over the lonely remains of the Nelson Railway, silence prevails.

After the rails had reached Glenhope, construction proceeded south towards Kawatiri, was halted in April 1913, and resumed again just before the General Election of 1914. All work ceased again in 1917, though little had been done since 1915 apart from a few miles of embankments.

In 1920 unemployed labour was used to drive the Hope Tunnel through the difficult granite, and foundations for the Hope Bridge were laid. By 1926, after workers had been brought from Otira, the line was opened to Kawatiri, but work to Gowan was suspended because of doubts over the economic feasibility of the line. A public outcry resulted in all the old arguments of rich mineral deposits etc. being bandied about once more so that in 1928 (again, coincidentally, an election year!) the line was extended to Gowan, some eight miles south-west of Glenhope, where a station was erected. After the Murchison earthquake work was again suspended, with the rails five miles further on past Gowan. In 1931 the track south of Glenhope was closed, and finally lifted in 1941.

The Nelson Progress League kept up a constant attack on successive governments. In 1935 it appeared that the new Labour

Top: Leaking valves allow steam to drift out in a cloud that almost obscures Ab748 as she prepares to leave Waitara with half of an overweight train for Sentry Hill, whence she will return for the rest of her train.

Centre: The author keeps an eye on the steam pressure gauge of Ab823 as he takes over for a spell of driving at Ross on the West Coast.

Bottom: This was the fireman's view from the Ab748 as the bucking, struggling engine tackled the grade out of Waitara in the great days of Steam.

Top: The laborious task of coaling up with air-powered crane and bucket is demonstrated by Ab817 and her fireman at Waitara in the last days of Steam in Taranaki.

Centre: The fireman gives the window a final polish while the driver and guard have a discussion, as Ab823 sits at Westport waiting to haul a short goods train down to Greymouth.

Bottom: Ab823 was busily shunting wagons at Stillwater when this photo was taken in January 1966.

Government might recommence work, but these hopes proved fruitless. The formation work on the line had reached within three miles eight chains of Murchison, and the League's immediate postwar object was the completion of formation work and the laying of rails to Murchison, a task estimated in 1930 by the resident engineer to take only 18 months.

Such efforts proved fruitless and in May 1954 the Government announced its intention to close the line in view of the heavy operating loss. Traffic ceased on 13 June 1954 but resumed on a goods-only basis four days later following representations and guarantees by the ever-anxious Progress League. These expectations were not fulfilled and 23 September 1955 saw the closure of the line.

The uplifting of the rails was accompanied by the demonstrations of some local women who, with a combination of the tactics of Gandhi and Mrs Pankhurst, passively and actively resisted the ripping up of the tracks; and there was bitter feeling on the part of some residents of the province. As an isolated section there was no justification for the continued existence of the line which had been losing money every year from 1911 onwards as the rails pushed deeper into the Murchison wilderness.

What the Nelson Railway's possibilities might have been can only be conjecture. There is no escaping the fact that many sections of the railways failed to pay until they were linked to the national network, as there is no escaping that many parts of the country, notably the central area of the North Island, were just wilderness until the railway came through. Many King Country towns date their foundation from the days when a steam locomotive whistle first echoed through bush and scrub that gave way to streets, houses, and people. As a trunk route it is possible that the Nelson Railway could have eventually paid its way. The Labour Government in 1960, shortly before the General Election, started surveys of a line to Blenheim but this was quashed with the change of government. So Nelson remains without its railway, to the financial advantage of the local trucking and bus companies. With the development of the mammoth Golden Downs Forest project and the possibility of a pulp and paper mill in the area, it is possible, bearing in mind the example of the Murupara and Kinleith lines, that a railway could again come to Nelson, albeit as another isolated section. That would indeed be irony of Gilbertian dimensions!

Many branch lines were built for the sole purpose of moving a

D

specific commodity, coal or timber generally, and where the supplies remain, these little lines still quietly go about their task of moving raw materials down to the main line railheads. One such example could be heard until recently, through the mist of a foggy Waikato morning, when the muffled thundering of a steam locomotive exhaust beat upon the air. A black shape accompanied by the surge of sound from a laboured exhaust and the rumble of wagons finally resolved itself into a little Bb class shunting engine, its eight coupled wheels slipping on greasy rail as it fought its way upgrade. It was the morning mixed train of the Glen Afton branch on its way from Huntly up to the mines that stud the nine-mile length of the Waikato's Glen Afton branch line. Until recently the Bbs with the help of an occasional Ab, worked all traffic on the branch, but the bucking Bbs have now given way to the smooth diesel efficiency of the Db, the smaller edition of the Da, and all traffic over the line is now diesel-hauled.

Of some consolation to enthusiasts however is the knowledge that the little locos of the Mines Department are still very much in the hunt, and a quainter collection of steam power is scarcely to be found anywhere else in the country. At the time of writing, an F class 0-6-0 tank, ex-NZR, could still be seen skittering into Rotowaro from the Taupiri Mine with a load of wagons, or waiting patiently in early morning sunshine with a train of three ex-NZR passenger cars of last century vintage, to collect men from the Huntly train to go up on the little private line to the mine. An 1876 vintage C class 0-4-2 tank engine could be spotted heading for the Renown collieries or, in more massive proportions, the 1927 Hawthorn-Leslie 4-6-2 Tank No 3 ex Ohai Railway Board might chuff importantly about the yard, as befitted her status as the youngest and largest private steam engine in the area. Here is a fascinating collection of steam antiquities all of which, oblivious of the fact that they can properly be regarded as museum pieces, blissfully chuff about their appointed tasks.

The Glen Afton line was authorised in 1910 for the sole purpose of exploiting the local coalfields, though there were optimists who hoped to see the line eventually extended to Raglan. It was completed to Pukemiro, a distance of seven miles, by December 1915, when the War prevented any further construction. The final section of under two miles, to Glen Afton, was built with sharper curves, and the grades average 1 in 50, requiring heavy earthworks, so that by 1922 there were three steam shovels working on the line. A unique feature was that much of the excavation work was done by the New Zealand Co-op. Dairy Company, owners of the Glen

Afton Mine, the only time in the Dominion's railway history that such an organisation constructed a Government railway.

Wet weather that gave considerable trouble with slips was responsible for delaying the handing over of the line to the Railways Department until 1924. A notable feature was the absence of the political manoeuvring and wrangling over routes that had accompanied the construction of most other branch lines, and the line has considerable goods and passenger traffic, in marked contrast to the generally prevailing branch line situation. Today the harsh throb of a Db echoes in the cuttings and around the curves of the Glen Afton branch, but for all that it is a line that remains well worth a visit by anyone with a yearning for the unusual.

Branch lines have written a fascinating chapter in the history of the New Zealand Railways, and many lines that merit space cannot, alas, be covered here. The last-century atmosphere of the Seaward Bush branch, the little lines that bravely head off to the Southern Alps, only to peter out at small settlements in the foothills, the sound of two Das getting under way with almost 2,000 tons of logs on the Murupara line, the chime of an Ab tackling the terrain around Motuhora with a train from Gisborne in happier days, these are or were the branches of the New Zealand Railways, some among the most modern lines in the nation, others now gone, or relics of a past of small engines, light loads, and wooden cars. They are rich fields for the discovery of gems of railroadiana.

5

On goods and through gorges

A TRAIN of open four-wheel La wagons, some sheep wagons, a few four-wheeled box wagons and a van, headed by a B or A engine. A total of perhaps 300 tons on the drawbar as the engine whistles out of the station and bounces off down the light (55 lb to the yard) rails, with her train banging along in tow. At a North Island station a Da's klaxon blares, the motor beats out its drumming sound of power and takes up the slack in its 1,000-ton train. The brakes ease off as the roar of the motor shouts up an octave. On a South Island night, a Ja or Kb puffs mightily, steam pours out of the cylinders in a white spurting cloud. Hauling long trains of Z bogie box wagons, some Uc bogie tank wagons, bulk cement wagons, Rb bogie open wagons, sheep wagons, cattle wagons, Kp box wagons for forklift loading, long low flat wagons with bulky loads and the longer Lc four-wheeled open wagons, they rumble off over 91-lb rails into the night.

Here's a study in contrasts between goods haulage in the old days, and the long, efficient, specialised freights of the railway scene today, where long strings of wagons snake around curves and the rumble of a train's passing may echo in the air of a frosty night for many minutes as it moves on through the darkness with the goods, materials, and products of a nation in tow. The life-blood of the railways is the goods trains, and without them the country would grind to a standstill.

Most of the railway goods traffic moves at night. Wagons are loaded during the day, and through the night they move on to their destinations at points all round the compass.

My first night trip moving the goods was Train 789 from Otira down to Greymouth with departure time around 9 p.m. J1216 was waiting on the loop with a long train of empties to go back to the mines and mills of the Coast. A wavering light down the line presently resolved itself into a J, staggering up the grade with a heavy load of freight for Canterbury. The red light changed to green and steam spurted into the cylinders as the driver eased out on his regulator. The couplings banged and crashed as the train rumbled out over the main points and off down the grade into the darkness – a darkness relieved only by the yellow beam of the headlight as it swept over bush and scrub, penetrated by the green glow of single-line automatic signals. Each light controls a section of track and if the section is clear, green shows for oncoming trains. They are controlled by the trains themselves, the engine circuiting a slight current in the rails which controls the colour of the lights. At one bend on the run down from Otira, such is the grade that no less than three signals can be seen simultaneously, the last a pinpoint of red or green far away and well below the vantage point of the locomotive.

With a light train and an easy run it was a pleasant trip in the warm summer night and the fireman stretched his legs while I took over his seat and called signals. The J was merely loafing with her train, and only the odd shovel of coal was needed to keep her with a full head of steam. Scenery naturally was invisible, apart from the immediate area illuminated by the headlight. Around Moana however it was a different story. A rising moon glimmered on the water of Lake Brunner, where a phosphorescent surge of water marked the skimming passage of a fast motor boat and the red glow of campfires, like the Coast glow-worms, glimmered and sparkled around the shore of the Lake. Campers came out of their tents and waved towards the black shape flickering fire and belching smoke that passed around the shore. The whistle blasted in reply to their greetings and echoed around the lakeside.

We drew into Stillwater Junction at 11.35 p.m. and ran the engine up under the waterspout. It is surprising how many Grey-mouth-bound engines suddenly find themselves short of water at Stillwater, only 10 miles or so from the loco depot at Greymouth. The very excellent reason is of course that crews are allowed 35 minutes for putting away their engine, involving fuelling, watering, greasing and so on, and if a longer time is taken the men are then working in their own time. Consequently, as the time saved is appreciable and the amount of water used from Stillwater is fairly negligible, a lot of thirsty engines arrive there!

At the same time the fire is raked to the back, the clinker and muck made ready to be dropped out over the ashpit at the depot, while the green banks at the sides are pushed well to the front and fresh coal is applied to the sides of the box. At loco the grates are dropped, and the remaining clean fire is raked over, fresh coal is applied, and the engine is ready with a clean fire for another trip.

At 11.45 we cleared the Stillwater main and curved off around the long tangent towards Greymouth. The lights of occasional cars came and went on the road beside us as the J eased herself and her train around the bends on the track beside the Grey River. Soon we clanked down on to the wharves at Greymouth, beside the black waters of the river, to uncouple from our train which would be left for the Ds on tomorrow's wharf shunt to break up. Backing off down on the crossover, J1216 headed wearily down to the roundhouse to be bedded before another day of serving the Railways, moving the coal, timber, and freight from the forests, mines, and factories, to their appointed destinations.

The following day I joined Ab823 at the head of Train 819, a light goods from Westport to Reefton and Greymouth. Ab823 was possibly the most spick-and-span engine I have ever been on, diesels and electrics included. She positively shone, having been only very recently outshopped after overhaul at Hillside Workshops. Her boiler was clean and sparkling, literally gleaming, no dust and grime marred her wheels, the only grease was the bare amount needed for efficient working rather than the great globs that seem to festoon most engines like flies on rotten meat. The sea-green painted interior of the cab was only just beginning to show traces of soot and it contrasted vividly with the bright red leather of the crew's upholstered seats. She might have stepped from the pages of a builder's catalogue, a picture of well manicured and coiffured locomotive beauty.

Her train was brief: a couple of wooden La wagons, a sheep wagon, and some Xa wagons, one earmarked for fish traffic, made up the light total. At 11.45 a.m. we pulled away from Westport as a shower of light rain swept in from the sea, splattered the cement ship and fishing boats at the wharves, and disintegrated on the gleaming boiler of 823 as she negotiated the points out on to the main line. At the Guardian Cement Company some bulk cement wagons were added to the consist, though the works were closed at the time and the usual busy traffic was a mere trickle. The line is easy going and almost straight to Te Kura where, shortly after, it enters the Buller Gorge, one of the most famous scenic attractions in New Zealand; photos of cars parked on the section where the road cuts through the overhang of rock are familiar to most people.

Thought of a railway through the Gorge above the turgid green waters of the eddying Buller River had long been discussed. Originally the Westport line was to have been a mere branch of the great concept of the Midland Railway Company's Nelson-

Brunner-Canterbury line. The failure of this grandiose scheme in time elevated its conjectural branch to a completed main line. As early as 1885, the Government had announced its intention in the matter, though it was to be another 20 years before "King Dick" Seddon turned the first sod on 22 January 1906. Despite the easy country, it took four years for the first six miles of line to reach Te Kura. Work was dilatory until 1915 when, due to the exigencies of war, it petered out altogether. For how long work might have languished had it not been for the Cascade Coal Company's mine a few miles on through the Gorge, is anyone's guess. The company was formed in 1926 and the following year the first wagons of coal clacked over the tracks from Cascade down to Westport.

The run through the Gorge is unfortunately not the attraction that it used to be. While greater stability has undoubtedly been given to the banks by the secondary vegetation, the bushes and trees do nothing to enhance the view; instead of breath-taking watery vistas of foaming rapids and placid green pools, the rail traveller mostly sees only ferns and young bushy trees. From Cascade the country is more difficult as the train swings and sways its way around curves, blasting through several short tunnels, along a cliff face, and over several short bridges to Titoroa. There a weed-covered crossing loop with a water-tower stands on a little flat area of land above the river which winds its relentless way through the rocky slopes.

The progress of construction was increasingly difficult as the rails advanced slowly on through the rugged gorge. The Depression struck the Westport line and work had to pause as the country tightened its belt and waited hopefully for the world to recover its economic sanity. By 1935 the Government was regaining confidence and investigation of the Gorge resulted in a decision to proceed with the completion of the line as quickly as possible. Fittingly, in view of the time that had elapsed since the first works were put in hand, and doubtless considering the general lack of progress made, a new sod was turned to mark the beginning of new work.

Notwithstanding the will to succeed, however, the line made very slow progress. Despite the use of advanced machinery previously non-existent, the formidable task of construction in such country had possibly not been fully realised. It was found necessary to encamp the workmen on the less cramped roadside and ferry them to and from the railway workings by boats or over suspension bridges. It almost became touch and go whether Hitler would emulate the Kaiser and force a halt to construction; but finally, on 2 December 1941, the last spike was duly driven and the Public Works Department began operating trains through to Inangahua until the Railways Department took over the line two years and three days later.

Trains through the Gorge are severely limited in speed by the curvature of the line, of necessity following the twists in the river. The average curvature is about 10 chains, though they go down to 7½ chains' radius in places. Ab823 was certainly not out to set records and the miles slid steadily if slowly by beneath the beating wheels as she made her way towards Inangahua. Some 90 minutes after our departure from Westport the train chuffed slowly across the unusual combined bridge over the Inangahua River, where road and rail run alongside each other instead of being inter-mingled as on the bridges south of Inangahua. The trip was not a hurried one, the combined bridges, some speed restrictions, all combined with a generous timetable, meant steady loafing progress down to Reefton, as light rain sprayed against the windows of the cab and mist swirled around the mountain tops. The Ab fussed around the yards at Reefton where some shunting was required, until after a belated lunch we headed south again and prepared to tackle the Tawai Bank.

The start was not auspicious. The now steady drizzle was greasing the track and the Ab spun viciously as we climbed away from Reefton. The Tawai Bank is a solid grade with the 1,234-foot Tawai Tunnel to be steamed through at the top. At the crest of the grade before the dip towards the Bank, the driver slapped on the brakes. Muttering that "the bloody shunters probably left on an extra wagon", he climbed down and anxiously surveyed the train to check that the tonnage had been decreased to the allow-able limit for an Ab up the Bank. All was in order, and he climbed back aboard where the fireman was throwing in the last scoop of coal to keep the needle on the maximum reading.

With a jerk the engine leapt ahead down the dip, swaying and bellowing as she hit the bottom and started the slog up the grade. The driver carefully notched back the cut-off, the wheels spun, gripped the sand being sprayed on the rails, and settled down to battle upwards. The smoke poured out and rolled away from the funnel in a swirling black cloud that would have done remarkable credit to a Union Pacific "Big Boy" on the Cheyenne Heights. Ahead was the narrow mouth of the notorious Tawai Tunnel, with its narrow confines a byword among Coast crews. The exhaust thrashing and echoing as sound waves rebounded off the walls, we dragged our way through in a maelstrom of smoke and heat that miraculously vanished as we came out into the open again.

At Tawai Station we took the loop and the opportunity to boil up, while awaiting the northbound railcar. Normally I'm a coffee addict but locomotive tea, I had to admit, was pretty good stuff. Water from the tender goes into the billy, the billy on to a rod, and the whole is thrust into the flickering wall of flame in the firebox. Presto, in about 20 seconds the billy is boiling. In go the tea-leaves, another few seconds and "Tea, Milord, is poured". Electric-jug manufacturers could well take instruction from an Ab. From Tawai it was an uneventful trip to Greymouth, through such solid sheets of rain as only the Coast can produce, until the welcome sanctuary of the Greymouth roundhouse, warmed by the heat from sheltering engines, replaced the cold showers still falling outside. It was a good place to be. . . .

For over 25 years the bulk of goods traffic in the North Island was hauled by the K and Ka classes, until the advent of the Da, now the mainstay of the North Island main lines. It was with considerable anticipation therefore that I looked forward to my first goods run on a Ka. It was a cold clear frosty night at Palmerston North, where stars were winking in the inky dome above, and steel ribbons were gleaming in the light of arc lamps which silhouetted the irregular shapes of wagons caught like moths in the harsh white light. Ahead loomed a great black bulk, wreathed in vapour, panting like an old dog after a hard day's mustering. Ka932, that I was to ride on a night freight to Takapau at the head of Goods Train 944. The train was a light one, some 300 tons in a total of 38 wagons that stretched away into the shadows behind the engine.

We left Palmerston North at about 8.30 p.m., to the solid *Whoof, whoof, whoof* that only the K classes' exhaust seems capable of producing, that exudes the feel of pent-up power waiting for the hand on the regulator to release it into the cylinders in a surge of force translated to the eight driving-wheels. There was a delay at the exit to the yards while we waited to cross a railcar but then, to the solid punch of a Ka taking the strain, we ground out of the yards on our way to Hawke's Bay. A quarter moon shed its cold faint light into the cab, blending with the muted glow of the dial lights as the warm smells of oil and smoke drifted in the windows. The steady note of the big engine's exhaust steepened in pitch as she dragged her train out on to the main and soon we were beating along steadily at a boneshaking 30 mph on the run through to Ashhurst. A combination of bad springing, no compensating gear and bad light track, meant some pretty rough running to Ashhurst, where after a wait for the CTC light to turn to green, we moved out for the run through the Manawatu Gorge.

The contract for construction of the Manawatu Gorge line was let to Messrs Jones and Peters in November 1886, some 300 men being employed on the construction works. In contrast to the Buller Gorge, work here was pushed ahead vigorously, and in 1888 as a means of unemployment relief in the Bush District, work was begun from Woodville as well. The construction was by no means as difficult, for the country was not as rugged as the Buller, but different problems were encountered. In contrast to the rock of the Buller, difficulty was found in obtaining firm foundations for bridges and retaining walls, due largely to the clay-slate rock found in the area.

It is just such rock that has ever since been a constant menace in the Gorge and a source of continual nuisance as rock-slides detach themselves from time to time and skid down over the tracks or into the river. On the eastern end of one of the two long Gorge tunnels a large extension had to be made to protect the tunnel against rock-slides from the slope above. The rock can be dangerous as well as an engineering hazard: in August 1946, Ka951, on the head of Goods 942 to Woodville, was struck by or hit a large boulder that had come bounding down the mountain-side, and the engine, tender, and several wagons pitched down the bank, killing the unfortunate locomotive crew.

It took a considerable amount of time and effort to raise the engine. Many of the external parts were removed, the boiler was jacked into a position whence it could be hauled up the bank, the wheels, frame, springs, equalisers, and brake gear were all brought up separately in an operation that took four months to complete. The damage to the engine, particularly from the effect of cold water entering the boiler, was such that it was almost a year before the engine was back in service again. The Gorge can be dangerous. . . .

While the Manawatu does not enjoy the lush bush-covered slopes that line the Buller, at least there is no secondary growth to obscure the view, often sheer down into the slow-moving green water below. On the opposite bank, as we jogged along, the flashing headlights of cars came and went as the light of the Ka swept around the curves, beamed across the river, flickered on the opposite bank and slid away again as the engine followed the curve of the track on to a new tangent. We clattered past what had once been a passing loop in the days when trains were more abbreviated than they are now, but the rails had long since gone, rendered useless by longer trains and more advanced signalling. The Gorge station too has disappeared, and there are now no crossing loops between Ashhurst and Woodville.

The fireman had knocked down the back of his seat and I sat leaning out the window watching the long black boiler silhouetted against the light of the headlamp's glare. The coupling gear was clanking out its musical rhythm, an almost jingling sound that seems peculiar to the Ka, and one that intensifies when the locomotive is drifting. We took the loop when we arrived at Woodville and dropped off a couple of wagons on to a back shunt. The yards at Woodville are new, and obviously built for the diesel age – our eight-coupled Ka stalled on one point curve that had been designed apparently for only the six-wheel truck of a Da. Woodville marked the then end of CTC and the stationmaster came over with the tablet that would permit us to enter the next section of line ahead.

We chuffed softly out of Woodville, past the old engine shed where a De, a Dsb and an Ab832 kept sleepy company, and as our smoke pall shot into the clear black night we headed round towards the north-east as the Wairarapa line turned away from us in the opposite direction. It is quite a steep haul out of Woodville, though as our train was 100 tons under the permissible weight the grade was no real problem.

The grade levelled out on to a long straight and the crew took the opportunity to sand out. The regulator was jerked open and the Ka kicked up her heels and took off in a flurry of sound, thick black soot-laden smoke jetting from the funnel, the clattering blast echoing around the sleeping countryside as the sound sliced through the chill still air. The drifting steam was condensing in the cold and fine mist drove against the window and splattered on my face as the rushing air caught the spray and whipped it back.

It is a common misconception that the footplate of a steam locomotive must be an oppressively hot place and there are times admittedly when this is certainly true. On other occasions there can scarcely be a colder, draughtier place, half-open to the elements, the wind whistling in the windows and out past the tender. Thick coats and scarves are essential items of equipment on a cold night. Despite two singlets, a thick woollen shirt, and two thick jerseys, I was becoming increasingly colder as the night wore on, the front half of me getting some warmth from the boiler backhead, the back half completely numb as the draught tore past my rear. As we freewheeled through little country whistle stops such as Papatawa, we could see the frost glinting white on the fences and paddocks along the line.

The line climbs most of the way up to Dannevirke, including a long winding upgrade north of Papatawa. The big engine was given her head, and with the sound of the exhaust beating out its challenge and defiance of gravity, load, and curvature, 932 literally bounded her way up. We levelled out and whistled through the little Maharahara Station, where once copper had been mined. The tablet was exchanged on the move, and the train clattered on through the night towards Dannevirke. The rail was better here and the ride more comfortable.

We reached Dannevirke at 10.35 and drew up to the frost-encrusted water-tower to top up the tender. There was no shunting to be done, but a crew change was to be made with a Wairarapa-bound goods headed by a Da, so we settled down in the chilly cab to await its arrival. Eventually the long train rumbled in and the crews changed over, the crew off the diesel, with its heated enclosed cab, spending some minutes struggling into overalls, scarves, and coats for their spell on the Ka. As the Midnight Special, the whistle blew a vibrant blast that crashed around the still town at five minutes past midnight to be followed immediately by the snorting panting effort that means that a Ka is getting its train under way on a frosty night.

North of Dannevirke the grades begin to steepen and become more frequent, and the beat of the engine's working heightens in pitch. North of Ormondville, the 6 mph speed restriction was observed over the Ormondville Viaduct, a long curving structure, 129 feet high, that had its foundations damaged in the Napier earthquake in 1931 and which has had a speed restriction on it ever since. There are several miniature viaducts north of Dannevirke, the country is hilly, and the line twists through between the hills as it wends its way like a river seeking the easiest course. At odd intervals were faded notices warning "K, Ka, Wab engines SLOW" – a relic of the past, because at the time of this trip most of the Kas had been scrapped and the other two classes had not run on the line for a considerable time past.

Finally, at 1 a.m. we drew into Takapau where train 941, on which I was to return to Palmerston North, stood waiting on the loop. It was time to reverse my tracks and head back on yet another of the New Zealand Railways goods trains that, unheralded and unsung, generally unseen in the black of night, perform prodigies of haulage for a nation that could not live without them.

6

Rambling in railcars

SINCE THE DEMISE of the steam-hauled provincial passenger trains the railway passenger transport field has been dominated by the fast red railcars that now traverse the country daily. The old mail trains were slow and inconvenient, and where once there was a daily or even perhaps a two or three times weekly express service, there may now be two, three or more daily railcar services at more convenient times. For many, the symbol of railway transport nowadays is the railcar, rather than a long string of carriages. In fact the only regular non-suburban passenger trains in the country are the Main Trunk trains of both islands, and the Masterton-Wellington workers' train which, in a man-bites-dog situation, actually replaced a railcar service.

The first railcar – if such it could have been called – was built in 1906 when a little D class steam engine was combined with a passenger car. This experiment with steam cars was not over-successful; the locomotive was wasted on such limited accommodation, and steam was not really seriously considered thereafter except for a short period in the mid-twenties.

In 1912 a little four-wheel petrol railcar was built and this can be considered as the remote ancestor of railcars in this country, breaking as it did with the concepts of steam haulage. There were several other experiments tried at this stage, and later, in an endeavour to provide a suitable railcar. In 1914 a Westinghouse petrol-electric was tried, and in 1916 a Thomas Transmission car.

By 1925 the situation was becoming desperate and the railways were badly in need of increased passenger accommodation. Within 12 months Buckhurst and Leyland petrol cars and Sentinel-Cammel and Clayton steam cars were being experimented with. The latter were designed for non-rush periods and to exploit passenger traffic on branch lines where motor competition was being increasingly felt.

The Clayton car as illustrative of the general types under consideration had an overall length of 55 feet, with steel underframe and a body catering for 57 passengers. The power unit was a standard Clayton road vehicle unit, a two-cylinder high-pressure type with all parts totally enclosed; the boiler, of the vertical water-tube type, had a working pressure of 230 lb. This unit was mounted on bearings on the forward axle of the driving bogie and a hardened steel pinion on the engine crankshaft drove a spur wheel on the axle. An exhaust steam water-heater was provided, with a coil superheater on the top of the boiler. The fire-grate was only 3·27 sq. ft and "little and often" was the fireman's rule.

The car with its geared drive could attain a top speed of 45 mph, scarcely a great rate by today's standards but quite reasonable for 40 years ago. Control cabins were provided at each end to dispense with the necessity for turning, an essential attribute for branch line service. Some of these steam cars gave reasonable service, but on one tried on the Hutt Valley line, trouble was experienced with the gear drive employed, and on the whole they cannot be considered as other than an experiment.

An Edison storage-battery railcar was tried out in 1926 and for some years was a feature of the Little River branch in Canterbury until it was burned in a fire at the Christchurch locomotive depot some years later. The car itself performed well but the task of battery charging was a tedious one and again the Department failed to come up with an acceptable solution to the problem that was besetting them.

In 1936 two little four-wheelers, Rm20 and Rm21, were placed in service between Christchurch and Hokitika. They were used for the Christchurch newspaper delivery to the Coast and were in fact subsidised by the Christchurch *Press*. In effect they were little more than a Leyland Tiger adapted for rail use. Powered by diesel engines they carried 19 passengers, or 13 with a load of papers, and covered several hundreds of miles daily until they were scrapped in 1942.

A small Ford touring car mounted on two pairs of wheels was tried out as an inspection car in the early 1930s. It made one memorable trip up the Rimutaka Incline, with frequent stops, much spragging of the wheels, and an assistant perched precariously on the bonnet with a bucket of water, to cool the engine. The experiments were enough of a success, however, to encourage the Department to build the famous "Wairarapa" railcars.

These cars were built in 1936 in an endeavour to speed passenger working over the Incline. They were scheduled to cover the 65 miles between Masterton and Wellington in under two and a half hours, where the mail trains could at best manage only three and a half to four hours for the journey. Initially they were fitted with a 120 hp Leyland petrol engine, mounted under the floor at a sufficient height to clear the centre rail. Because of a possible fire risk they were re-engined in 1938 with diesel motors. The Wairarapa cars were of special lightweight construction and seated 49 passengers, with a front bogie and a single pair of driving-wheels towards the rear.

The first test run over the Incline was made by Maahunui and there were some very anxious moments indeed at times. The weather could hardly have been worse: icy winds howled around the snowcovered mountainside and whipped scatters of snow across the iced tracks. The car was weighted with sacks to simulate passengers. At Siberia the car began to skid and slide on the ice but spragging gear was quickly brought into play and her skid was fortunately arrested. The trials were extensive ones and were not always smooth sailing. At one stage a song was written (to the tune of *Daisy Bell*) a verse of which ran:

> *It's rougher than ten years' marriage*
> *This rattletrap railcar carriage,*
> *There's far more room*
> *And much less gloom,*
> *On a bicycle built for two.*

The Department however was justifiably proud of its new cars and sent them on extensive show-the-flag tours. Arai-te-Uru for instance, was the first train to make the through passage from Wellington to Wairoa. A contemporary journalist described the Maahunui as "This handsome new landship ... Majestic, stately, shining in the sunlight, it approached like the gorgeous howdah of some eastern Potentate." Fulsome praise indeed! – and not entirely undeserved either. There was no doubt that the "big" cars made a tremendous impression.

For the Wairarapa railway traveller they came as a godsend. They were fast little machines and it was not long before the downgrade from Pigeon Bush to Featherston became renowned. To gallop down here at more than 60 mph with a howling southerly pushing at the rear was indeed an experience. The cars revolutionised passenger traffic over the hill. They could climb up at about 15 mph which was three times as fast as any train could manage, and the long, severe grades and curves on the Upper Hutt side of the hill did not slow them as much, though the journey was always made to the protesting squeal of flanges as they screeched around curves. After 1948 no more passenger trains were scheduled and thereafter, except for specials, the cars bore the brunt of the traffic.

A companionable atmosphere, almost like that of a suburban bus, prevailed on the Wairarapa railcars. The driver's controls were not screened from the entrance vestibule, which meant that anyone who travelled reasonably frequently soon came to know the drivers as old friends. Though officialdom might frown on such happenings, my father on several occasions after business trips to Wellington was set down at our back fence, which adjoined the main line. I have spent several enthralled hours sitting in the spare side seat beside the driver while we ground over the hill, trundled through the Manawatu Gorge, or flashed across the South Wairarapa Plains.

The cars had a personality all their own which was helped by the fact that they were all named (after Maori canoes) – Mamari, Mahuhu, Maahunui, Mata-atua, Arai-te-Uru, were some whose names I recall with pleasure. With the exception of No 9 which, I seem to recall, was chocolate brown, all were painted red though without the striping now borne by railcars.

Nowadays slick 88-seaters make light work of the Wairarapa run in a standard of comfort that far exceeds the best that the little cars could manage. For anyone unfortunate enough to be seated towards the rear of a tin hare (as the little cars were nicknamed) over the single driving axle, the ride was rough indeed. The enraptured contemporary journalist previously quoted, in a paroxysm of excitement during his first ride, wrote: "There is the feeling of being on a magic carpet. Nothing seems to be producing motion; the scenery is simply slipping by."

Most people who travelled on the Wairarapa cars would probably suspect the anonymous writer of having been fairly fully in his cups at the time, for the cars were frequently referred to as "square-wheeled little sods". To sit in the rear on the run down from Pigeon Bush was frequently to virtually invite physical injury in the form of a snapped neck. Nevertheless, whatever their rear-end shortcomings, their speed, their personality, and their friendly crews, won them a special place in the hearts of the travelling public, and it was not without regret that many people said farewell to them in 1955.

After the success of the Wairarapa railcars, the Standard types were built and these were also named, Aotea being the first of her type built. Large, heavy, double-bogied cars, seating 48 passengers with cabs at either end, they were more comfortable and easier riding than the tin hares. They handled for some years the New Plymouth-Wellington run, and had a distinctive silver livery before this was changed to the familiar red because of complaints that they were too difficult to see at level crossings.

The Standards are the oldest surviving railcars in the country, and still retain some of their old original dark varnished wood trim, their sloping fronts a reminder of the streamlining passion that gripped railway engineers before the last War. They are still great old cars to travel in, the view from their huge windows being unbeaten by any other passenger vehicles on the railways. Unfortunately not all the seats line up with the windows, and the less fortunate must be content to contemplate the pattern on the wall trim for the whole of their journey.

The Standards have a most distinctive engine note when at rest; the whole unit sounds as though it is disintegrating in a rattle of flying pistons. Once under way however there is no misunderstanding. The Standards, for all their age, are capable of some sustained high-speed running. At 65 mph the ride is smooth and apparently effortless as the mileposts whip past in a streak of white beside the racing wheels. Nowadays, after a period of years on the Napier line in addition to Taranaki, they still give sterling service on the Wellington-New Plymouth line.

The next railcar development was in 1940 when the Vulcans made their appearance. To me it is a matter of regret that with these cars the Department broke with the practice of naming their railcars. Nowadays they are just "railcars" – whether No 58 or 102 does not matter much. But how much more interesting it used to be, to see that our car was Tainui, Tokomaru, Mahuhu or my personal favourite, Mamari. What were merely railcars became individuals endowed with a personality by the simple expedient of providing them with a name. Today's policy is an unfortunate one; it appears to display a lack of concern, yet the use of imagination in regard to such small details can attract members of the travelling public. After all, "named" trains have always had an aura all of their own.

The Vulcans are by repute the most comfortable railcars in service, though as my experience of them has been mainly confined to the driver's compartment I am not particularly well qualified to comment on this aspect except to say that they do seem to be extremely steady riding vehicles. They first entered service in 1940 and delivery from the Vulcan works in England was completed in 1942 with the exception of one that was lost at

E

sea in a torpedo attack. Initially they were placed on the
Christchurch-Hokitika paper runs but gradually spread to Westport, Timaru for a time, and the Otago Central line. Their bogie-
mounted engines of 250 hp (275 overload) work through a five-
speed gearbox to provide a top-gear speed of 75 mph. The driving
bogie is four-wheeled, a centre carrying axle distributing the weight
of the motor.

Their light (9 tons) axle loading was very useful on the light
track to Reefton and in 1942, with the opening of the Buller Gorge
railway, Vulcans began through services which they still undertake
today. It was a run from Greymouth to Westport that gave me my
first experience of these fine cars. I travelled on the jump seat to
the right of the driver on Rm58 on the early morning run with
departure from Greymouth at 7 a.m. The Coast railcar morning
runs are still primarily newspaper runs, and there were few
passengers but many newspapers when we left Greymouth. The
track is light and ballast fairly sparse to Reefton, and although a
Vulcan once officially attained 78 mph on the Midland line, and
unofficially has for instance run the 26 miles from Dunsandel to
Christchurch in just over 19 minutes, the maximum was 50 mph
on this occasion, and in the main the average between-stations
speed never rose above 40 mph. Rm58 in company with another
Vulcan had once had a brake failure in the Otira Tunnel and
finished up derailed at the end of the runaway track at Otira, but
on this occasion the trip was quite uneventful apart from the
hurling-out of newspapers, including one at the Australian-sound-
ing locality of Snake Gully! Dad and Dave, however, were not
anywhere in evidence at the time.

Of all the trips that can be made by railcar, perhaps none is so
beautiful as the daily Vulcan run from Dunedin to Alexandra.
The service goes up at night and leaves Alexandra at 7.20 the
next morning for one of the most spectacular runs in New Zealand
through the wilds of Central Otago where the grey rocks sprout
like mushrooms from the sun-coloured tussock. Past the towering
massif of the Rock and Pillar Range they go, through cuttings
between solid clumps of rock, and over the several viaducts
beneath which the tinkling waters of mountain streams lap around
their boulder-strewn courses. The Taieri Gorge is a railway and
scenic attraction exploited all too infrequently. Clinging tenaciously
100 feet above the swirling waters of the Taieri River, through
tunnels whose unlined rocky walls look like the interior of giant
rabbit burrows, to descend to run beside the meandering river as
it curls its way through the rugged canyon, the line is like an

advertisement for the Canadian Pacific Railway. Whether you're a geologist, a railway enthusiast, or a tourist, a run through the Taieri Gorge by Vulcan is an experience not to be missed.

At present, the ultimate in railcar travel is the Drewry Car Company's standard 88-seat articulated which has done much to revolutionise railway passenger transport. The first time I saw one of these fine machines was when the Prime Minister and official party travelled to Masterton to mark the opening of the Rimutaka Tunnel. It must be admitted that the newcomers and their Dg class companions of the goods-hauling breed made a favourable impression upon those who had been used to the tin hares and some rather grubby A and Ab class engines. A much accelerated schedule was introduced with the opening of the Tunnel, though at first there was considerable difficulty experienced with the Fiat engines, which were prone to overheating. There was even a team of Italian experts sent out to assist. However the new service began to settle down and the travelling public were quick to appreciate the relative luxury of individually-adjustable reclining seats and the increased riding capabilities that three bogies gave. The 88s may have lacked the breakneck thrills that the Wairarapa types provided, but they surely were worlds removed in comfort.

The articulated 88-seaters are of interesting construction. The body and underframe have been built as one unit which has the effect of forming a hollow beam. Two of these beams are mounted on three bogies, the middle one being a carrying bogie. As they are frequently operated in multiples of two or three, a seating capacity of up to 264 can be provided. The disadvantage of multiple operation though, is that while only one driver is needed, at least one guard must be provided for each car, there being no intercar access while in motion.

On most runs, overall average speeds are in the vicinity of 30-35 mph, the curves and gradients so frequently encountered rendering any higher speeds very difficult. The Christchurch-Dunedin service probably gives a truer indication of their potential, where for 230 miles an overall average of over 40 mph can be attained. When it is realised that this includes some 16 inter-mediate stops, the between-stations running is required to be vigorous. The power that pushes the 88s along is contained in two underfloor mounted Fiat 700.040 horizontal six-cylinder diesel engines with a total rated output of 420 bhp at 1,550 revs. The top geared speed is 65 mph though I have been in the cab when the needle was rock-steady at 70 mph and the motors were not extended in the slightest.

The delivery of the cars was disappointing; originally due in July 1954 the first car could not be test-run until November of that year. They first entered regular service on the Wellington-Gisborne run, and greatly increased traffic resulted from the daily service that replaced the five-day-a-week express train. When the Department introduced the cars there were great plans for them, and in my opinion it is a great pity they were not carried to fruition. It was planned that the 88s would operate a daylight service between Wellington and Auckland, and the estimated schedule was only 11 hours for the 426 miles of the Main Trunk. What a tremendous service it could have been! Morning and afternoon tea was to have been served by hostesses, eliminating wasted time at refreshment stops and providing amenities it is certain would have been greatly appreciated by the travelling public as a whole. What a revolution in railway transport it would have been indeed.

My first cab trip on an 88 was from Woodville through to Palmerston North on Rm101, the second of the class. After some exhilarating 65 mph running in an endeavour to make up time, the 25 mph speed restriction through the Gorge was a bit of an anticlimax. The compartment has a seat for the guard, but enthusiasts travel sitting on the fire extinguisher.

After squally weather, we had burst into sunshine at Woodville and the trip was delightful as we banged our way around the bends above the river far below, sparkling in the sunshine. The 25 mph speed limit was carefully observed, because the Department was having a blitz as a result of an engine sideswiping a tunnel wall when travelling faster than authorised. Once out of the Gorge speed increased and we had a faster run to Ashhurst where a Da sat throbbing impatiently, waiting for us to cross. On the straights into Palmerston North a steady 55 mph clipped off the mile pegs until we swung around into the fast growing Milson industrial complex and on into the orderly maze that is the Palmerston North goods yard. A bewildering complexity of wagons, shunters, shunting-engines and scattered Das flashed by until the brakes shuddered on and 101 drew gently to a halt at the No 2 platform.

The 88s now travel over a considerable portion of the New Zealand Railways tracks daily. Travel between Gisborne and Wellington, Rotorua-Auckland, Wellington-Woodville, Picton-Christchurch, Christchurch to Ross, and to Dunedin, to name a few routes, has been revolutionised.

Fine as the 88s are, I doubt however whether they can yet be regarded as the last word in railway passenger travel. It must be conceded that most of the provincial expresses were hauled by Abs only on fairly generous timetables, and were subject to curvature and grade restrictions more severe than generally exist now. The railcars are generally more prone to sidesway than carriages and can become uncomfortable at certain speeds. They also suffer from luggage restriction. One of the big advantages of train travel used to be the large amount of luggage that could be carried, but this has retreated in the face of posters appealing to railcar travellers to limit their luggage requirements.

The Masterton-Wellington workers' train also proves the point that with modern motive power, the train is not necessarily slower. This train when De powered required almost two hours to get to Wellington and was generally late most nights in arriving at Masterton. The De is about equal to an Ab in good condition, and the lesson becomes obvious when it is realised that the 6- or 7-total train, now Da powered, is timed to eclipse by eight minutes the railcar schedule over the same route.

The 88s are useful, fast machines, but they are not in all respects superior to the express train, which has unfortunately never been developed in New Zealand to its full potential. Perhaps the ultimate answer will be midway between the two, the diesel train, a (say) four-unit bogie-powered train with cabs at each end, rather like those in service in Europe and Japan. This would combine the compactness and speed of the railcar with the increased capacity, weight, and comfort of the express train, while being able to provide a more luxurious standard of travel. The 88s are a fine vehicle and a great improvement on their predecessors, but are still somewhat utilitarian when compared to other forms of transport not necessarily much, if at all, more expensive. With greater comfort and a few more frills, the diesel train or a heavier railcar could do much to woo passengers back to the rails again.

7

Rimutaka reminiscences

ONE OF THE MOST LEISURELY train trips possible used to be that over the Rimutaka Incline in the days of the "Fells", before the Rimutaka Tunnel was opened and the Wairarapa yielded to the diesel conquerors. It was possible to climb the hill on foot faster than the snorting, panting little Fells could manage. To have ridden on an "express" up the incline was to have tasted one of the more unusual samplings from the varied world of steam.

The Incline was justifiably world-famous among rail fans. It was the only really successful and longlived application of the Fell principle in the world, and as an engineering achievement it ranked high in the global list of railway wonders. From its inception it was never really intended as anything other than a temporary measure to be replaced eventually, when funds permitted, by a more economic and practical line of railway to the Wairarapa Valley. Almost from the time the Incline opened there were plans for better and easier alternatives, but it was to be 80 years before the tunnel through the Rimutakas replaced the Incline.

Under Julius Vogel's public works policy the Rimutakas were surveyed by John Rochfort in 1871, acting under the supervision of John Blackett, then the acting engineer-in-chief of the New Zealand Railways. Rochfort, one of the giants of New Zealand's early railway survey and construction days, ended his report with the laconic comment: "In conclusion I may say that my party were the first Europeans who have travelled this route." What volumes of hardship are compressed into that simple sentence!

Initially three routes were considered: one by the road saddle, one around the coast, and one using the saddle, 1,444 feet above sea level, discovered by Rochfort. The coast route was dismissed as impracticable. The road route presented tremendous difficulties in construction of earthworks and curves. Finally the saddle route was chosen, with a summit tunnel lowering the height to 1,141 feet. Investigations were made over a period of 12 months as to the best method of descent to Featherston. Relatively easy graded lines would, it was found, involve eight or nine miles of descent, with curves of three chains radius and 19 tunnels. So it was that the 1 in 15 descent to Cross Creek was decided on.

Fixed winding engines were at first proposed, but investigation brought the obvious conclusion that the curvature of the track made such a system impossible. It was then that the Fell system was approved, the system of inside, horizontally-inclined driving-wheels, gripping a horizontally-inclined, flangeless centre-rail. This had been developed by Englishman John Fell from the original design of two European engineers, Messrs Vignolles and Ericsson in 1830.

In 1877 the first Fell engine entered service, and three more were introduced in 1878, the year that the slim steel rails reached Featherston. Amid the thunder of artillery salutes, the jubilation of the local citizenry and the frightened screams of small children and horses, the railway arrived in the Wairarapa. Two more Fells were placed in service in 1886, to cope with the increased traffic following the opening of the line to Masterton and to the Forty-Mile Bush.

My most vivid recollection of the Incline is of one warm day in spring, October 1955, on one of the last trains over the hill, an excursion from Masterton to Upper Hutt and return. We enjoyed a moderately paced run down the valley which was shimmering in the warm sunshine, and the air echoed to the tread of our Ab as she passed by in a cloud of steam and aging dignity. We rattled through Featherston, passed Pigeon Bush, and eventually arrived at the little township nestling amid the golden gorse of the foothills – Cross Creek – to generations of railwaymen, simply "The Creek", no other elaboration was necessary. A collection of railway houses bravely sporting wind-battered flowerbeds, a station, yards, engine shed, hall and – always – gorse. This was The Creek.

Up ahead at the end of the yards could be seen the raised centre-rail that had made a Wairarapa railway possible. An ominous reminder of potential danger was the runoff track, a long length of track on to which a train whose brakes had failed on the hill could be diverted and on which, it was optimistically hoped, the train would eventually stop before running into the stopbank at the end – this was always assuming, of course, that the runaway managed to negotiate the bends on the way down, which was, to say the least of it, problematical.

The passenger arriving at Cross Creek was greeted by the sight of four or five ponderous little 0-4-2 tank engines with extraordinarily complicated running gear, wheezing and panting loudly as they awaited the incoming train. On arrival at The Creek, the train was broken into sections and reshunted, with one of the little engines spaced at approximately every three carriages. The Fells could each cope with a maximum of 65 tons up the incline, and to ensure that each engine pulled its load and to avoid undue strain on the drawbars, they were spaced accordingly. With a shrilling of whistles, some half hour or more after arrival at The Creek, the train charged the grade.

The sight of a train beginning its climb was staggering. It appeared almost as an optical illusion. It would literally charge the grade at what looked to be quite a speed, yet by the time the second engine had bitten into the centre-rail, the speed was down to a walking pace, as if some giant hand had firmly grasped and slowed it. Wheels slipped and exhausts broke rhythm as the little locomotives fought for adhesion and traction. The peaceful October day was shattered as the roaring exhausts echoed around the scrub-covered hillsides. Smoke from five diminutive engines shot 200 feet up into the radiant blue of the mountain sky. As the grade increased, so did the noise, while the speed was with effort maintained at a comfortable walking pace. You could leave the leading carriage, hike 50 feet up the hill, and after taking a photo, rejoin the last carriage at the same spot where you had left the train. On this particular occasion the carriages were festooned with streamers, fond chalked farewells adorned the sides of the cars, and happy excursionists watched the gorse slide slowly by as the panting engines inched their way upwards. The tunnels on the line must have been sheer hell for the engine men. In the carriages it was bad enough: thick, choking, sulphurous, dirty-yellow smoke swirled around the cars and within seconds formed an impenetrable curtain of pea-soup all about. It leaked in at the doors and the cracks around the window-frames, and the pungent odour soon permeated everything.

For the men in the last engine, Dante's Inferno would have seemed like an ice palace. The cab of the Fell was almost certainly the most uncomfortable of any engine on the New Zealand Railways. It was very hot, even when standing, and so cramped that the fireman could wield what was virtually only a fireside shovel.

Service at The Creek was regarded by many railwaymen as a form of penal servitude, and many men were in fact frequently banished there for misdemeanours. One driver of my acquaintance who had doused a rather dishonest insurance agent with a steam hose was told: "There's a railcar for The Creek at seven tomorrow morning – you'll be on it!" This driver did three months at The Creek and escaped eventually by volunteering (it was 1939) for each of the Services in turn. He left thankfully for the War in the first that accepted him. Other men loved The Creek, and some spent almost the whole of their working lives at this remote and at times inhospitable locomotive depot.

Another driver, however, told me that the tunnels were no problem – if it was a goods train with some box wagons in the make-up. The trick used by some drivers was to open the sander slightly, ensure a good head of steam, and drop from the engine when the tunnel was nearing. A quick sprint and both men would throw themselves into a box wagon, roll the door shut and then, when the tunnel was ended, spring out and rejoin their engine. It was obviously a dangerous practice, but one that no one who has been on the footplate of a Fell would grudge them.

At Siberia we passed the windbreaks that were erected after the fatal accident in 1880, in which three children were killed and six adults injured when a carriage and wagons were blown off the line. So strong was the wind on that occasion that the fireman had to crawl up the hill for help clinging to the centre-rail to avoid being himself blown down into the gully. But there was no wind on the day of this trip, and the mountain valley down which roared the occasional screaming banshee, looked calm and innocuous on such a fine spring morning.

After some 45 minutes of solid climbing the engines panted wearily into the summit tunnel, and the clanging of a bell in the subterranean darkness told us that the centre-rail had ended. A moment later we burst out into the sunshine at Summit, 1,141 feet above sea level and 869 feet higher than Cross Creek. Once again there was the long delay which no one minded while the train was split and the fussy little engines shunted to and fro preparing to pick up the northbound excursion train from Wellington. A pair of smart De class diesels, resplendent in red and cream livery, hooked on to our train and began the run down the 1 in 35 grades through the bush to Upper Hutt, to the protesting scream of wheel flanges on the tight curves.

On the return trip in the haze of the late afternoon, we set off down the hill again to The Creek. This time the little four-wheel brake-vans were interspersed through the train, with their trained guards manning the big counter-weighted wheels that applied the brakes to grip the centre-rail and control the speed of the downward train. On one of the last trains over the hill, an engine blew its valves, lost steam, and became a deadweight. The increased tonnage then being braked threw a severe strain on the brake-vans. Eyewitnesses later reported that some passengers had to be recruited to help hold the brakes on in the vans. Some anxious moments passed until the speed was held, and there were some relieved brakemen who saw The Creek loom up that night! One guard, of a rather generous build induced by rich living washed down with copious draughts of good brown ale, had to be carried off the train and lost several pounds in weight as a result of the adventure. It was indeed fortunate that the last days of the Incline were not marred by what could have been a terrible tragedy.

The last days of The Creek and the Fells were exuberant ones and yet tinged for many with sadness. The last excursion trains were gala affairs, jammed with excited people, many of whom were sampling the adventure of Incline train travel for the first time. Many no doubt had already made the trip by railcar, but there was no comparison between the faster uphill grind of a railcar, and the shouting efforts that accompanied an express, however much more time might be wasted. For many years our family had set their watches every morning by the whistle of the A class loco-motive that brought up three carloads of school children from The Creek to Masterton. "Hurry, there's the school train," was a familiar cry each working day. The closing of the Incline brought to an end the life of this little train, known to railwaymen as the Arawa. Its name derived from the old Rm10 railcar named Arawa which used to do the run before the numbers became too great. The bus transport that replaced the train was universally con-demned by the pupils as a lesser form of transport. A series of photographs of the last train now hang in the halls of Wairarapa College, the sole memorial of what had been an institution for many.

The Rimutaka Incline was an unusual and highly fascinating railway, but it was grossly uneconomic and extremely difficult to work and maintain. The story of the struggle to replace it starts as early as 1871, when Rochfort condemned the alternative coastal route. In 1897 detailed surveys were carried out by C. N. Knorp with the aim of eliminating the heavy grades. The pressing reason was the large number of passengers being lost by the Government to the new Wellington & Manawatu Railway Company. Of the 12,439 passengers who arrived in Wellington in 1897, only 777 came by the Government line. The Government of the day did everything it could to encourage traffic away from its competitor, and the Department charged less for wool and livestock to Palmerston North, Longburn, Feilding, and Marton farmers, than to those in the Wairarapa. The Prime Minister, Richard Seddon, described this state of affairs as one of "friendly rivalry" and was immediately taken to task by the *Evening Post* which in its issue of 7 January 1898 had this to say: "The premier is constitutionally incapable of making any statement as to public affairs that is consonant with facts excepting when it suits his purpose."

The paper continued that the encouragement of traffic over the incline was "ruinous competition" and "having all the appearance of a deliberate breach of faith".

It was in this happy atmosphere that the surveys for an alternative route to what was proving a severe embarrassment were pushed ahead. Knorp suggested the construction of a 1½-mile long tunnel with grades of 1 in 40 through the ridge above Abbotts Creek. Nothing was done in the way of construction, but surveys abounded, and a map of the Rimutaka Ranges showed the snaking lines of many other proposals and investigations, all of which came to nought.

In 1908, with the acquisition of the Wellington & Manawatu Company's line, the pressure eased dramatically, and it became the practice for consignments to stations north of Masterton to be run up the coast and through the Manawatu Gorge as a cheaper alternative to the Incline. Before 1908, up to 130 men had been stationed at Cross Creek, and it was a bustling hive of activity, trains pulled by up to four Fells and We377 or 198 were a common sight. Even after the traffic fell away, there were seldom fewer than 35 men including 20 locomotive men. Besides the depot at Cross Creek it was necessary for crews to be stationed at Upper Hutt and Masterton, three depots in 64 miles of line! Three separate engines (taking the Fells as one) were required to move a train from Masterton to Wellington, and the coal consumed in taking a train the three miles up the Incline would equal the amount used on the rest of the Masterton-Wellington journey.

Despite increasing agitation for alternative routes, the Department for several years experimented with modified locomotives in the hope of speeding traffic and avoiding the enormous capital expenditure that an alternative route was obviously going to cost. The first two engines adapted for use on the incline were the W class 2-6-2 tank locomotives which worked trains on the Incline as assistants to the Fells until they were transferred in 1901 and 1904. The We class were rebuilt as 4-6-4 tank engines from B class 4-8-0s and in 1902 were assigned to Incline work. Though they were officially considered a success, they were described by a former locomotive man in an article written for the *Wairarapa Times-Age* as "at best a makeshift". The driving-wheels were unnecessarily high at 42½ inches for the slow speeds and sharp curves, and some difficulty was experienced in maintaining the water-level in the long boiler, a circumstance that did not trouble the stubby little Fells.

Of all the engines built or rebuilt for Incline working, however, none acquired such notoriety as E66, the infamous "Pearson's Dream", described by engine men as "the most hellish thing ever put on a railway track". She was built at Petone in 1905, at a cost of $14,000 and with eight cylinders, two exhausts, and 12 drivers, was a modified "Mallet" articulated. It was essentially a spare-parts locomotive, using spare cylinders from N and O class engines, and driving-wheels from F class locomotives. The intense heat from her Vanderbilt corrugated cylindrical firebox was her worst feature, and the asbestos leg-pads supplied to her firemen have passed into history. The brute certainly had power, 29,000 lb of tractive effort, and reputedly once hauled 120 tons up the Incline, but she was so reviled whenever she worked in the Wellington area that by 1917 she had been scrapped. Her name appears to have come from a verse composed by a Thorndon cleaner C. W. Foster, who wrote:

> *E sixty-six, what a box of tricks,*
> *The result of an engineer's dream,*
> *Believe it or not, she's so flaming hot,*
> *She turns your sweat to steam.*

Meanwhile, agitation was not assuaged by these various experiments, and in 1913, 1920, 1922, 1924, and 1930, full-scale deputations representing the Wairarapa converged on Wellington led by pipe bands and skilled orators, seeking relief from their cumbersome railway. In 1920, Prime Minister Massey promised "a good time coming". In 1922 he said he hoped to have the first sod of a new deviation turned by 1923, and anticipated the work would cost $2,000,000. In 1924 the press reports of the deputation convey the indignation that was being felt, and the chairman told the Prime Minister, who by now must have been a well-known acquaintance, that this biennial deputation could not go on much longer, that something would have to be done.

The final deputation in 1930 was promised that the matter

would be referred to a Royal Commission which doubtless did nothing to enliven the once more fruitless journey back home over the Incline. Besides the major deputations, countless letters to editors, chambers of commerce deputations and press editorials railed against the Incline and pressed for alternative measures. By 10 June 1938 all this agitation had apparently achieved its purpose, when the Government announced that it would proceed with a Mangaroa-Cross Creek tunnel. The jubilation was short-lived, because the outbreak of War in 1939 brought preparatory work to a halt.

At the War's end the Incline again came up for consideration and over the next two years six different routes were surveyed which culminated in April 1948 in the decision to construct a 14-mile deviation between Upper Hutt and Featherston, involving two tunnels, one of 27 chains and the main one of 5 miles 37 chains, the latter coming out in Lucena Creek, near Pigeon Bush – oddly enough a gully that had earlier been considered as a possible route via Lucena Pass.

The Ministry of Works began driving the main tunnel in 1949 pending contracts being let to tunnelling firms. The contract went to the San Francisco firm of Morrison, Knudsen for a price of $4,590,670. A New Zealand firm, Downer & Co, were also associated with the work, which began at Mangaroa in June 1951 and at Featherston two months later. The Mangaroa face was driven at an average rate of 84 feet, and the Featherston end at 120 feet, per week. In the main, the full-face method of drilling and firing a full round was used, involving mucking out, timbering, and then a repeat of the process. The older heading-and-bench method had to be resorted to at times though, when weak rock was reached. The modern methods used enabled completion of the job in 16 months less than the contract allowed, and in one week on the Featherston side, a world record 250 feet were tunnelled in one week.

On 23 April 1954 the first "train" of wagons carrying officials travelled through the tunnel taking, with two derailments at crossing loops, some two and a half hours for the journey. Fortunately this was no indication for the future, and normal mainline speeds are now allowed through the tunnel. The new deviation incorporated the flash-butt method of welded rail tracklaying, and lengths of 117 feet were laid, with 351-feet lengths inside the tunnel itself. Considerable difficulty was experienced in the track-laying due to a shortage of men and extremely wet weather conditions, but finally all the problems were overcome, and on 3

November 1955, the then Prime Minister, S. G. Holland, declared the deviation officially opened and – as at so many other similar ceremonies – the rain poured down steadily as he did so.

Fittingly, the old Fell No 199 was present at the Speedy's Crossing ceremony and quite stole the show from the immaculate Df that had hauled the official train through the tunnel. Equally fittingly, No 199 now stands preserved at Featherston as a memorial to the sterling work she and her sister locomotives performed.

With the tunnel came a new era in locomotion in the Wairarapa. Overnight the faithful As and Abs vanished, and residents whose houses abutted on to the line and who had been lulled by the soft chuffing of a night goods, awoke to the harsh roar of a diesel pounding by with a long goods train. The Wairarapa had become New Zealand's first dieselised railway. The Des and Dgs have now been replaced, except for the odd De-hauled shunt, by the larger Das, whose growling roar as they attack the Opaki grade with a long freight can be heard for as long as 20 minutes as they get through-goods trains on their way. What the Ab was to the line in pre-Tunnel days, the Da is today, even if local residents do evidence less interest in their passing.

After the opening of the tunnel, the old Incline was quickly taken up, and various clearing sales of equipment were held. Much of the Fell rail went to the West Coast for use on the Rewanui and Roa inclines, while with the exception of 199, the Fells finished up on a siding at Silverstream and were quickly cut up under the blue flames of acetylene torches. Cross Creek, having been increasingly neglected as the Incline's final days drew to a close, collapsed in final desolation and demolition.

Today, only the metal roadbed, a gangers' hut and gaunt chimneys around which the wind moans, mark The Creek. Some smoke-blackened timbers lie where once Fells, As and Abs weathered the long winter nights in the warmth of the Cross Creek loco shed. There are no more children to travel on "the school train". No rails, no sleepers, no wagons, no engines – no life. The once bustling, vibrant, existence of The Creek is gone and will never return. Gorse is slowly encroaching on the denuded roadbed as it winds its way up the hill; soon it will be covered for ever.

But on lonely nights when the wind howls up the valley and around the tunnel mouths, perhaps then the valley echoes once more to the phantom panting of little engines, dragging ghost trains up the mountainside on the line that for 80 years they served so well.

8

The growlers

IT IS A COMMONLY HELD FALLACY, no doubt heartily supported by diesel locomotive manufacturers, that the diesel is "new", "the latest thing", "the *modern* locomotive". In fact, Dr Rudolf Diesel (acting, according to diehard steam fans, under the guidance of Satan himself) patented his first "rational heat engine" in 1892 and farsightedly predicted its suitability for use in ships and on railways. A British patent had even been granted to one H. A. Stuart two years earlier for an engine working on similar principles. Had the name stuck, steam enthusiasts might now have been berating Stuarts instead of Diesels.

Strictly speaking, diesel engines should probably be called compression-ignition engines, because unlike petrol engines, no spark is needed for combustion. Only air, as opposed to air and vaporised petrol, is drawn into the cylinder and this is compressed to the extent of 500 lb per square inch or more. The great pressure raises the temperature of the air to a point where the injection of fuel results in ignition without any spark.

Originally, the big problem with Dr Diesel's engines was their bulk. They were extremely weighty and appeared suitable for accommodation only in large units such as ships. But for this problem, the diesel age on the railways might have already been with us years and years ago. Improved technology saw these problems combated and overcome, and led to the increasing sophistication of these engines. Nowadays railway diesel engines may be of several types, usually distinguished by their cylinder arrangements. They may have four, six or eight cylinders in line, or eight, 12 or 16 in Vee formation, as many as 12 horizontally opposed, or in line, vertically opposed or in line, or the unusual arrangement used in the 3,000 hp Deltic engines of British Railways: these latter (which are not represented in New Zealand) are in the form of an inverted-triangle cylinder arrangement, whereby each side of the triangle is a cylinder containing two opposed pistons with a crankshaft driven by two of the cylinders, in each corner of the triangle.

In all cases, of course, the power of the actual engine must be transferred to the wheels or the locomotive will never get anywhere. Diesel locomotives use three main forms of transmission: electric, hydraulic, and mechanical. The most common transmission now employed is diesel-electric, the form used in all main line New Zealand diesel locomotives. The diesel-electric is nothing more than a mobile generator, the diesel engine providing the power for the generator, which produces electric current supplied to electric traction motors on some or all of the axles of the locomotive.

The hydraulic system, after initial serious problems, is now beginning to come into its own, albeit slowly, and is gaining increasing popularity in Europe, where the German firm of Kraus-Maffei is to diesel-hydraulic what General Motors is to diesel-electric. The hydraulic drive uses oil or similar liquid as its medium and makes use of the principles of a centrifugal pump or impeller driving a turbine. The final drive is achieved by shafts to the axles. There are no representatives of this type of transmission in New Zealand.

The remaining type of diesel locomotive is the simplest, where the diesel engine itself drives the locomotive directly, generally by means of side-rods to coupled wheels, using a clutch and gearbox. Railcars and shunting locomotives generally use this type of transmission which, because it is less flexible, is not favoured for heavy-duty work.

So much then for the diesel engine itself, but its application to use on rails is something that, like the development of the engine itself, has not been as dramatically rapid as was the development and the application of steam to railway use. A diesel-electric railcar was put into service in Sweden in 1913, and after the First World War a number of European countries began to turn to diesel-powered railcars. In the 1924-5 period, diesel-electric engines appeared in Italy, Tunisia, and the United States, the American engines being forerunners of the well-known Alco "switchers" (shunters). In 1925 also, as a result of 15 years of advocation, a combined Russian-German produced diesel-electric of 1,200 hp went on trial. This proved to be the most successful of three other 1,200 hp designs using mechanical, pneumatic, and hydraulic transmissions. Only the electric and mechanical transmissions proved successful at that time.

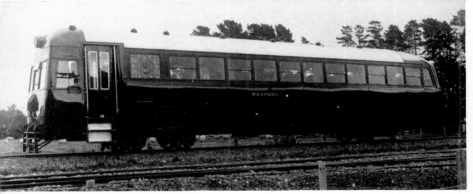

Top: It's late at night and most people are asleep; but for Ka935 and her crew it is just another night's work as a southbound freight waits for a crossing at Levin in the last Ka days of the Trunk. A steam loco at night was an unforgettable sight. . . .

Centre: *Maahunui*, one of the lightweight Wairarapa railcars used on the Rimutaka Incline, poses for a formal portrait. The "tin hares", as they were known, gave a good account of themselves for nearly twenty years.

Bottom: *Tokomaru*, one of the old standard railcars which still give good service to the NZR, takes a spell at Taumarunui between runs.

Top: Officially the fastest ra[il]cars in New Zealand are t[he] Vulcans. Here Rm58 has j[ust] arrived at Westport on t[he] morning run from Greymou[th]

Centre: A familiar sight [all] over New Zealand are [the] Drewry railcars. Here t[wo] coupled in multiple are se[en] waiting to cross a train runni[ng] in the opposite direction.

Bottom: "Time for refres[h]ments at Masterton!"—and [Ab] 758 gulps water on a hot Fe[b]ruary day in 1964. She w[as] working a goods from Woo[d]ville whose diesel had fail[ed.] Once a familiar sight, stea[m] has not been in regular serv[ice] in the Wairarapa since 1955

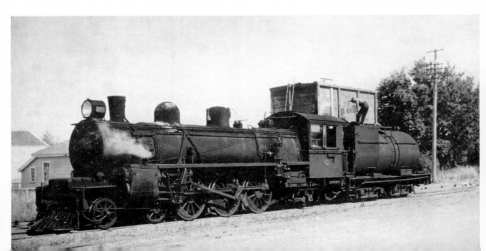

In 1928 Canadian National Railways operated the first high-powered main line diesel-electric in North America when they put into service Canadian National No 9000, a 2,660 hp machine which tipped the scales at a massive 334 short tons. It was a bold step on the way towards efficient diesel traction.

Diesel's next big occasion was in the 1930s when the Reichsbahn (German Railways) developed their impressive diesel railcar and train sets including the Flying Hamburger and the Rheingold Express. The development in the USA in 1934 of the Chicago Burlington and Quincey Railroad's Pioneer Zephyr really set the seal on diesel success. The Zephyr introduced the high-speed lightweight engine which had been lacking in diesel development at that date, and the then popular concept of streamlining, for which diesels were more easily adapted than steam, ensured their acceptance by the travelling public. The Zephyr's 1,015 mile nonstop run averaging 77·6 mph on 18 April 1934, was something that steam, for all its reliability, could not match in regular service. It may well be argued that on that date the writing appeared on the wall with a brush dipped in dieseline. From then on, the acceptance of diesel power, which had hitherto been a novelty, became fact.

New Zealand has always been in the forefront of railway development, no matter what the attitude of the average New Zealand citizen to his railways may be, and investigations had been made at a very early stage of diesel development. Only one year after America's 1925 switcher had been developed, New Zealand was considering diesel traction for use in the Lyttelton Tunnel. A special study was made abroad in 1929 when P. R. Angus, later to become Chief Mechanical Engineer, decided that the diesel locomotive was still too close to a mere experiment to be adopted for use in New Zealand. The final seal of success on diesel locomotion abroad, however, was the comparison made in the United States between steam and diesel during the years of the Second World War and immediately following, when it became obvious that the American Railroads intended to stake their money on diesel traction. In 1935 there were 113 diesels in service in the United States. Twenty years later there were over 21,000, the majority built after 1945.

The experiment was over; and in 1948 New Zealand, having already had considerable success with her diesel railcars, set about ordering small batches of diesel-mechanical and diesel-electric shunting locomotives and, two years later, her first main line diesel-electrics.

F

The first locomotives ordered came in 1949 and were four diesel-mechanical shunting engines of 204 bhp designed by the Drewry Car Company of London. Classified Ds and Dsa they commenced work in Wellington yards and, apart from the expected settling-down period, gave good service. The settling-down process however tended to be a little wearying for crews, and in desperation, on more than one occasion, the fireman was known to have sat in the shed keeping a C or Ww in steam ready for the expected SOS from his mate!

One driver is reputed (at a time when one-man control of shunting engines was envisaged) to have told a brass-hat: "It is absolutely necessary to have two men on a Ds."

The brass-hat replied soothingly that the Department considered a fireman unnecessary on a Ds. The driver glared. "Who the hell's talking about a fireman? I need a *fitter* to keep the bloody thing mobile!"

At some depots Dss were expected to cope in the initial stages with more work than they could handle, and had to be replaced by Abs at times when the work proved too heavy for them. There are now five different types of shunting engines of the Ds, Dsa, Dsb, and Dsc classes working in New Zealand, and they have revolutionised shunting methods. The Dsc class are diesel-electrics not diesel-mechanical, and were designed and built in New Zealand; they have proved that New Zealand, if she so desires, can build diesels from scratch.

By 1948 the experimental stage was well past overseas and the English Electric Company received New Zealand's order for 15 diesel-electric locomotives classified De, which arrived during 1950 and 1951 and were the first diesel-electric engines to be employed on the New Zealand Railways. Instead of being used for the yard duties intended for them, they were placed in suburban service in Wellington and Auckland. Later they hauled trains on the new logging lines in the Central North Island, and following completion of the Rimutaka Tunnel, goods trains on the Wairarapa line.

To some extent the De followed traditional steam outline in having the cab at what was obviously intended to be the rear of the locomotive. It was clearly more practical to run in "reverse" with the cab leading, to gain the advantage of the excellent window space in the cab, but crews who had been used to having many tons of locomotive boiler between them and anything they hit, were at first very reluctant to run in such an exposed manner. However, in time this attitude changed and as often as not, cab leading is now the fashion. With 660 hp the De would have made an admirable job of heavy shunt work, or of short branch line trains, but instead they were expected to cope with main line traffic, usually with a single engine. As such they were far from an unqualified success and grossly underpowered for such duties. On suburban trains they were almost never better, and often worse, than the old steam engines they replaced, and my experience with them on Wairarapa trains was little short of miserable. With five wooden cars they crawled the whole way from Upper Hutt to the Tunnel, some nights losing anything up to 20 minutes on the trip to Masterton.

Two years later, New Zealand was ready to try the big engines and in 1950 orders were placed in Great Britain, again with the English Electric Company, for 1,500 hp diesel-electric locomotives of the double-cabbed variety. Originally 31 were ordered, but subsequently only 10 were built, the others being in effect split into 42 Dg class engines. All 10 were built at the Preston, Lancashire, works of English Electric at a cost of $148,000 fob each. They developed 1,500 hp, weighed 111 tons and were designed for speeds up to 60 mph. They are powerful machines developing over 40,000 lb tractive effort and were put into main line service on the North Island Main Trunk in 1954 and 1955. Their settling-down process was, as might be expected, at times chaotic. Almost Gilbertian situations developed as valiant efforts were made to assimilate these monsters into the existing operational framework.

Train Control operators were instructed to "keep the diesels moving" and at the expense at times of virtually every other train on the Trunk, this was done. On time trains ran late while late trains were made later. The unprecedented situation developed on occasions where the Express and the Limited were stacked up on sidings to let Df-powered goods trains rumble through ahead of them. The Limited was known to have been held for 15 minutes at an unscheduled stop while a Df goods went on ahead. This was a far cry from the days when a delay of one minute on the Limited once meant that a report had to be on the General Manager's desk by 9 a.m. next day. Some diesel-hauled trains were running seven or eight hours late at times on the schedules that had been laid down for them, and among the loco crews it was bitterly commented that "somewhere in the employ of the Department we have former jet aircraft pilots arranging schedules".

The novelty of these engines did not soon wear off. The unprecedented sights of traffic managers handling the dog watches and stationmasters arriving at all hours to see the Department's new iron horses rumble through, were common. Some older drivers complained that steam-hauled trains were being deliberately side-tracked to give their crews the edification of watching a Df grumbling through. In five days in one week crews waited a total of 49 hours for Df-hauled goods No 199 to go past.

Finally, the Department was forced to admit that the Df, while an excellent locomotive, was not quite the super-engine they had tried to make it, but merely a perfectly competent locomotive that was being flogged past its limit. Schedules were altered accordingly, so that by October 1955 the schedules had sorted themselves out on a more satisfactory basis.

The Dfs, too, had not initially received unqualified approval from the men who operated them. One serious complaint was the lack of visibility caused by the large headlight, and after many complaints from the Engineers', Firemen's and Cleaners' Association, the headlights were eventually replaced by smaller ones. A lack of headroom and storage lockers, and insufficient heating were also complaints that the Department was forced to rectify. Once these minor matters had been sorted out, however, it was clear that working conditions on the diesels were certainly cleaner and more comfortable than on the steam locomotives. Goods schedules were drastically re-organised and "through" diesel goods with steam-operated shunts became the order of the day on the Main Trunk.

The 21 "split" Dfs were built, as previously mentioned, into 42 Dg class locomotives of 750 hp. The idea was to introduce more diversity into the diesel fleet. It was obviously ridiculous to waste 1,500 hp on a train that could be as easily hauled by a 750 hp locomotive. With the use of multiple-unit working, two or three Dgs could be operated as one unit to give the necessary boost in beef needed for longer trains. The Dgs have proved to be very useful locomotives in service and did not give as many problems as did the Dfs in their initial operation, largely as a result of course of the Department's experience with their Df runnings.

The Dgs provided the heavy power on the Wairarapa line in 1955, when this stretch of track became New Zealand's first fully-dieselised railway. They also worked the Murupara line for a time, before moving up into the Northland area where some of the class are still working. At the time of writing variations of the Dg, the Dh, are based in Dunedin and handle goods trains, as well as the South Island Limited over the Oamaru-Dunedin sector where they are more suited to the hilly nature of the country than are the faster Ja steam locomotives. The Dh has a variable axle loading, arranged by adjustment of springs between the bogie and the springbeam, which puts more weight on the driving-wheels, and all these engines can be reconverted to Dgs.

In 1955 came the first examples of the locomotive class that bids fair for reliability, numbers, versatility and sheer usefulness, to become the diesel equivalent of the Ab. This is the General Motors-built Da class, and with over 100 in service and more on order, it is now the most numerous class of main line engine of any type in the country. The first 30 were ordered in 1955 at a total cost of $3,590,000.

No less than 14 firms tendered for the order, including British, American, Canadian, Belgian, Italian, and Australian manufacturers. The General Motors tender was the lowest received in terms of traction horsepower, and the first locomotive was due from the works in 150 days from signature of the contract, and thereafter one every three working days. As two factories worked on the order, this meant two engines every three working days. This was about four times as fast as the Baldwin Locomotive Works delivered the ten Aa class steam locomotives (in 60 days) back in 1915, long regarded as a minor triumph of construction. Announcing the order, the then Minister of Railways, J. K. McAlpine, said that the locomotives were urgently needed to meet the demands of increasing traffic. It was expected at the time of ordering that they would haul heavier loads at higher average speeds, and over a given period would run twice the mileage of steam locomotives.

Whatever they may lack aesthetically, the Das have certainly lived up to the hopes of the Railways Department. They are virtually a standard General Motors "Road-Switcher" type unit, and needed very little modification to adapt them to New Zealand conditions. The cab roof had to be constricted slightly, but otherwise only the wheel gauge required alteration. Similar units have been exported to dozens of countries throughout the world. The Da was New Zealand's first hood unit, but all others since have been of similar design and the streamlined diesel is a thing of the past, utility rather than looks being the prime requirement in railroading today.

The Das are large and powerful brutes. Their 12 feet 2 inches of height is 8 inches more than what had been the previous maximum, and tunnel floors on the Main Trunk had to be lowered to accommodate them. Their diesel motor is a standard 12-cylinder engine, with wet-sleeve vertical cylinders, and known as the 567C type, developing 1,425 hp, probably the most uni-

versal diesel motor in railway use today. This engine generates
current to the traction motors whose horsepower output is 1,310.

The Das have revolutionised train movements in the North
Island where they operate. They had remarkably few problems
in settling down and the successive orders that have followed over
the years have been fully justified by the excellent operating record
of these locomotives. Right from the start of their service life they
have been a popular locomotive with crews and there were few
complaints such as had initially been made with the Df. From the
crew's point of view they are clean and comfortable, involve no
physical strain at all in their operation, and in fact it has been
recognised that they are conducive to sleep and have had to have
appropriate vigilance devices installed to overcome this! The
reaction of one driver to my query as to the merits of his Da:
"Just a bloody great chunk of steel with windows in it," is hardly
typical.

One of the few problems that arose in the operation of the Da
was the fear of crews that with the long hood leading (i.e. the
cab towards the rear with the diesel motor itself ahead of the cab),
there would be a danger of diesel fumes entering the cab. Exhaus-
tive tests were made by the Department which proved conclusively
that such fears were completely groundless. One of the supposed
advantages of the hood unit as opposed to the cab diesels, or steam
engines, was that they could be operated in either direction with
equal facility. In fact this did not prove to be quite the case.
Though the units could be operated long hood leading, the controls were really arranged for the other direction. The complaint
regarding the controls was admirably summed up by one driver
who likened it to driving a car in reverse, while sitting in the back
seat facing to the rear. It is now almost universal practice for hood
diesels to be run short hood first and turntables are as active as
ever they were in steam days. It has also been traditional for the
driver to be on the right-hand side of the cab, which is reversed
with long hood leading.

More than any other locomotive, the Da sounded the death
knell of steam power. Its performance was just too good for the
aging North Island steam engines to hope to match in anything
other than sheer speed with lighter trains. The sustained beef of the
Da is now the mainstay of heavy freight traffic in the North Island.
Lighter secondary power has now become necessary with the
withdrawal of the last Abs and Js from the North Island and to
cope with such traffic a smaller version of the Da, the Db, a 950
hp modified General Motors G-8 type, has been placed in service,

initially in the Auckland area, though it appears likely that as time passes they will be seen further afield and in increasing numbers.

For South Island traffic, the new Di class English Electric hood unit has appeared. They are an interesting locomotive, developing just over 1,000 hp yet with an axle loading of only 10½ tons which will give extreme versatility of operations as compared to the heavier diesel locomotives already in service. It is also the first three-axled bogie locomotive in New Zealand to have traction on all three axles of each of its two bogies.

At the time of writing, the first whispers of a further new diesel, the Dj, were being heard. Rumour has it that these engines will have the low short-hood type of construction, a compromise of cab and hood designs giving great visibility and now used almost exclusively for the design of the newer breed of American diesels, on which design most New Zealand diesels are patterned.

Whatever the future holds in store, the New Zealand Railways will have plenty of new locomotives to cope with it. Much multiple-unit running will doubtless be necessary to overcome what may be regarded as a tendency to rather low-powered units, when the overseas trend is now leaning away from the 1,500 hp multiple engines, to larger single units of the 2,000-3,500 hp range. By and large, the story of diesel development in New Zealand has been a successful one. The future appears equally promising.

9

Diesels from the footplate

A GREY MORNING AT TAIHAPE in January 1965. A long train of freight occupying almost the whole length of the station yard, over 60 wagons loaded with more than 600 tons of goods stretched from the guard's van in the distance, to the looming, reverberating bulk of Da1413 at the head of the train. The great motor grumbled monotonously as I made my way down the track towards the engine, which was some distance from the platform. It was Train 243, a Main Trunk goods to Palmerston North, and I was about to see diesel in action from the footplate for the first time. I swung up on to the running board and entered the cab.

The contrast with the footplate of a steam locomotive is startling. The first impression of steam is of suppressed power oozing to be set in motion by the application of some of the maze of control units that appear to stud the backhead in random confusion.

In stark contrast, the diesel cab is simplicity itself. Two seats, one of which sits nakedly by itself on the left, the other with a large "box" beside it with some gauges and switches, a lever or two, and blank walls all around. The cab is clean and quiet, only a subdued *chug, chug, chug,* from the motor penetrating the cab when the engine is idling. This is the latter day crewman's workplace. For the observer, the diesel cab is not as good as the steam footplate, for the fireman's seat has no let-down back, and on this trip it was a case of standing until a disused fire bucket rusting outside the Marton engine shed could be commandeered for better use.

The CTC light ahead flickered from red to green and the Klaxon blared, the brakes were released, the engine note suddenly changed from a low rumble to a sharper pitch as the driver moved the throttle forward and we wound slowly out of the yards on a leisurely run to Palmerston North. The beat of the engine was steady as we rolled round the curve out of Taihape, the train stretching around out of sight as the van cleared the yards and the four-wheeled La and Lc wagons bumped and clattered along, subdivided at intervals by the bulk of a bogie-wheeled Z wagon. There was no doubt that the Da was quite untroubled by the tonnage dragging at her rear. The engine appeared to be merely coasting along with no apparent effort at all. This was modern-age railroading, and for all its steady efficiency there was simply no comparison with the roaring power and straining effort of the steam locomotive.

We rumbled our way into No 10 Tunnel, 1,378 feet long, and the working conditions of the diesel became immediately apparent. No choking smoke eddied into the cab, no heat seared our flesh, no orange glow gleamed on sweating faces. The only indication that we were in a tunnel was the beam of the headlight cutting through the darkness and the increased thunder of the motor echoing off the confines of the tunnel walls. It was a steady trip, the engine forging steadily onwards at a regular 30 mph, coldly and surely devouring the miles southward. We passed through little country stations without pause, the CTC lights showing the all clear. Deserted railway houses all along the line are eloquent testimony to the staff savings that CTC has made possible. No longer do two or three men do shifts to work the signal levers and exchange the tablets. One man sits in a room and watches lights move on a board, and operates every siding and signal on perhaps more than 100 miles of line. There are some disadvantages though, where again the human touch has been ousted by mechanisation. In the old days a goods train crew could pick up a few minutes on schedule, and expend the time gained in gathering mushrooms. Nowadays Train Control will want to know why the light on the panel stopped for several minutes; crews must now buy their own mushrooms or go without!

At Mangaweka we had our first stop, but there was no running up to the water tank; the crew simply changed with a northbound goods waiting in the loop, and in a matter of minutes we were rolling south again. The cab of a hood diesel with its excellent forward, side, and rear visibility is a great way of seeing the countryside, whether it be the massive viaducts with the engine curving round off the Mangaweka as the rear of the train is advancing on to it, or the green bushcovered slopes and valleys through which the goods winds its steady way, through Hunterville down into Marton and on into the northern Manawatu.

We reached Palmerston North at 2.30 p.m. It had been a singularly uneventful trip, a typical piece of steady if unspectacular freight movement in the present-day workhorse of the North Island railways. One of my drivers had been a self-confessed steam man and at the end of the trip the remark uppermost in my mind was his comment: "I'd never work for the railways today if I was a young fellow. Thirty years of driving diesels would drive a joker mad."

This trip had certainly done nothing to counter that view, and it has been surprising how often old steam men have echoed it. In the South Island diesels are liked as an occasional rest, but not many crews seemed to be looking forward to working on them full time; and North Island drivers still speak of the Ka with a lingering note of wistfulness for the exuberant steam days that have now gone for ever.

It was some two years and many hundreds of miles of steam footplating later, that I again found myself in the cab of a diesel. This time it was the leading engine of a brace of Dgs, 755 and 767, which were waiting at Picton to haul Train 112, the overnight "express goods with car" that runs to Christchurch every night except Saturdays. Despite the official designation, the train was almost an "express with wagon attached" as we made ready to leave Picton. There were three carriages, a goods wagon, and the guard's van as at 8.40 p.m. the engines growled out of Picton and immediately set to on the long, steep grade that curves up around the hills out of the town. The engines were in notch 10 and steadily ground their way around the curves, rumbled over the Waitohi Viaduct, no longer an old timber trestle but a graceful concrete structure, and in a matter of two miles they had climbed 236 feet to the little whistle stop of Elevation, before gathering speed down through the fast deepening dusk of evening.

The Dg is a comfortable locomotive to ride. Up in the cab the visibility is excellent, the driver sitting in the centre, the fireman at a lower level on the left, and persons such as myself perching on the right-hand window-ledge. The Dgs, with the assistance of the new Di class (at present numbering three) now handle all services north of Kaikoura, though two Abs at Kaikoura, and further south, two more at Waipara, still handle several trains south of Kaikoura. The Ab class used to handle Train 112, and though they had to be worked hard, they gave an excellent account of themselves for many years. The Dgs still maintain the same schedule, though without quite the same effort on the part of the engine crews.

As we drifted down towards Mount Pleasant, the vigilance device, with which the Dg has only recently been fitted, emitted its usual whistle. The fireman punched the button, but the whistle kept sounding. Next moment the proverbial all hell broke loose. On a Da, if the device is not cut off, a hooter blows a steady solid note. On the Dg it sounds like an Irish club bar on St Patrick's Night. The whistle honks, squalls, whistles, hoots, in a mad uneven caterwauling that even the stone deaf would have some trouble sleeping through. In the confined cab it was ear-shredding. Fortunately whatever had been causing the trouble was rectified and the mad tumult died away to allow what seemed then like the quiet whisper of the motor to take over.

We breezed along beside the main highway near Blenheim, the driver dipping the big headlight for the oncoming cars on the road beside us, a gesture that they must surely have appreciated, for the double vertical headlights of the Dg illumine a long stretch of track when full on.

At Blenheim we shunted on four more box wagons, though in the busy season up to 20 may be picked up to make up the 400 tons allowed on the train. The cab of the Dg is fitted with a water cabinet and immersion heater and we took time off for a brew-up as we were well ahead of time with our light load. The motor of the front engine was shut down so that we could have our cuppa without its constant roar in the background. The train load was still very modest at only 223 tons as we notched our way out of Blenheim, and the two Dgs had no trouble rattling along at 50 mph over new track south of Blenheim, until with a shuddering crash we rocketed on to light 55-lb rail and the engines swung viciously over the rough old rails.

Train 112, and its northbound opposite number, Train 111, date back to the early 1950s when a train carrying vegetables ran from Blenheim to Christchurch between November and April. Later, about 1952, a car-van was added to provide a passenger service, and 111 was put on to provide a service in the opposite direction. At first, loads were limited to 180 tons, but the Abs performed so well that gradual increases in loading were allowed. The car-van was hardly the epitome of comfort; if placed at the rear the passengers froze, if coupled to the engine to allow steam-heating the light vehicle became almost airborne at times!

Nowadays the standard of comfort is good, with older first-class cars at second-class fares, and now, oil-heating-equipped cars with special seats, rather like those in first-class cars, that provide an extremely good standard of comfort at a very modest price. With frequent use being made of the service, the future of passenger travel on 111/112 seems assured.

Fourteen miles from Blenheim we passed through Riverlands and began the long slow climb up over the Dashwood Pass, while over to our left a bright glow indicated the lights of Wellington as we ground slowly upwards, around the almost 180° curve of the "big fill" and through a narrow tunnel whose walls bore ample evidence, in the form of scars, of some over-gauge loads that had passed through. The Dg may have lacked the heavy thud, bellowing exhaust, and clang of shovel that was an Ab crawling over the Dashwood, but it was still an impressive effort as the motors churned at top pitch while we crawled on through the night. It is five long miles at a 1 in 53 grade over the Dashwood, and the engine has to work every foot of the way. In steam days an Ab with a full load on wet rails could take nearly two hours sometimes to fight its way over.

Through the Dashwood Tunnel we thundered, the engines roaring and vibrating in the tunnel, along whose walls could be seen the gouges where Train 111 had crashed only a matter of some months earlier. Finally we staggered up to the overbridge on the state highway that marks the crest (at 510 feet) of the grade, and began the long drift downgrade towards Lake Grassmere, whose great salt piles glistened white in the faint light of a quarter moon.

There is some rough running in places on the North line, which at times seems so lightly ballasted as to resemble a private siding. A great deal of work has already been done by way of elimination of some tortuous curves, and more work is planned, as with the ever-increasing use of the Cook Strait rail ferries, the line becomes subjected to heavier traffic than could ever have been envisaged when it was first constructed. At 50 mph we dashed on through Ward, once a big locomotive depot in the days of the Wfs, and then slowed for a speed restriction before the motors once again blasted the blue exhaust forth as we took the Tarbarrel Hill. Soon we were blasting through Wharanui, terminus of the Picton line from 1912 until 1942, when after a tremendous effort, the two isolated sections, Picton-Wharanui and Addington-Parnassus were completed by December 1945, despite the fact that the country was deeply committed to wartime expenditure.

Little remained at Wharanui to indicate its past status. After the line had been completed it was important for many years as a banking and reduction station. As far north as Wharanui the ruling load was 700 tons, but it reduced drastically to 240 tons north.

For many years every train north had to be banked, but the more modern Dgs used in pairs have eliminated much of the shunting, and with two engines coupled in multiple, banking is, as it were, already built-in. The Dg rides well at speed and we bored on at a steady 50 mph until slowing for the famous "Blue Slip". This is a hillside composed entirely of blue pug, a very unstable material consisting of soft mudstone which, when saturated with water, moves very easily. Despite enormous amounts of material that were removed over the years, the slip gave trouble in equal amounts. It now appears to have finally settled, and has given little bother over the past few years.

A few yards away to our left the soft white lines of breakers splashed on the beach, while far off at sea the lights of the inter-Island steamer moved steadily southward, though she had a straighter and flatter course to follow than the Dgs had to contend with. Soon our speed through the night was slowed as we drummed over the Clarence River bridge, where a temporary trestle still served to replace a span washed out six months before. Away to the south we could see the lights of Kaikoura as the train snaked along the coastline, the sea a sheet of silver beneath the moonlight in the clear night sky. The Dgs were practically driving themselves, cruising along with only an occasional alteration to the setting of the controller, at a steady 45 mph, well within our scheduled timing. The brakes hissed on at Kaikoura at 12.10 a.m. and 755 was uncoupled ready to be hooked on as assisting engine to Train 111 which drew in a few minutes later with 18 wagons and three carloads of sleepy passengers.

At five past one, 767, now in sole charge of the train, shattered the air with the blast of her motor, and once more we rolled southwards through the night, first at a moderate pace, but soon increasing, with bursts up to 55 mph on the easy, curving run along the shoreline south of Kaikoura. Many of the 20 tunnels on the line are curved, and the headlight swept round the concrete walls where water droplets glistened momentarily before being swallowed up once again in the dank blackness of the tunnel. Moths flickered and danced towards us like tracer bullets, and an opossum sat transfixed by the twin yellow eyes until a dull thump announced that the 'possum menace had been reduced by one. The white clay of several small slips slid by beneath the rattling wheels, a reminder of the uncertain nature of the country we were traversing. In No 3 tunnel, telltale red clay marks, like boils, disclosed the cracks in the tunnel wall where the hillside had moved slightly.

At Hundalee the crew who had come off 111 at Kaikoura changed again with a Christchurch crew off a Di powered goods, and we headed off into the grades to the south. Once more the exhaust noise split the air as in notch 10 we chugged slowly up the Hawksford Bank until speeding up again through Parnassus and slowing for the half-mile-long bridge over the Waiau River south of the town. Shortly after, the Dg was again whacked up through the notches as she took the long straight grade up the Phoebe Bank. Once down the other side it was up to 50 mph as we surged on through the darkness past the spot where the little station of Nonoti used to stand.

The story may be apocryphal, but it is said that when Richard Seddon was asked to name the station, he replied: "No, not I." And so up went the nameboards – Nonoti!

The night ticked on as we rolled southwards, and after reaching Ethelton the speed began to fall as almost continual curves and grades hampered our progress. Clouds began to flit across the face of the moon, and soon the only illumination was the yellow light of the headlamps as a pale star flickered from time to time through increasing cloud cover. The darkest hour, it is frequently said, is just before dawn, and at 3.30 a.m. as we struggled up the Scargill Bank, only pitch blackness could be seen from the side windows. The steep climb was apparent in the angle of the cab, as in notch 7 we crawled along at 9 mph, a long, slow, tedious haul relieved only when we reached the crest at last. Dawn was lighting the sky as at 3.55 a.m. we pulled out of Omihi after changing guards with a northbound goods. Soon it became possible to distinguish trees, hedges, the shades of different paddocks that swept by, as we neared Waipara and moved out of automatic signalling into a tablet-controlled area.

We were well ahead of time, and ambled leisurely along at 40 mph, changing the tablet on the move as we passed through Amberley. It was obvious that the Dg, with such a load, was simply laughing at the timetable, and it was necessary to choke back even further to keep within our times. At a smooth 40 mph the miles slipped by, so smooth was the ride, that even half-asleep as I was at 5 a.m., it was no trouble to keep my feet in the gently swaying cab. We galloped through Belfast, where the freezing works were beginning to stir for the hard day of work ahead of them, and at 55 we rocketed through the Papanui Station and on into Addington. In the distance the Port Hills were covered in soft mist, while red, green, and amber signal-lights blazed ahead like decorations on a Christmas tree, no less than 21 being visible in coloured complexity as we swung down the line, to coast smoothly into the Christchurch yards. The hands of the clock flicked to 5.15. Another load of goods and passengers had safely arrived at their destination ready for the new day that would soon be upon them as a sleeping city slowly awoke.

A few days later I was once again on the diesel footplate of an express goods, but no longer in the South Island. By far the fastest land transport service between Auckland and Wellington is the express goods trains, Nos 630 and 631, that run each way Sunday to Friday most nights of the year, running the 425 miles in a scheduled 15 hours 30 minutes southbound, and 15 hours 48 minutes northbound, with overall average speeds on favourable sections of over 40 mph. The term "overall average" of course includes all stops, and while the maximum official speed is 50-55 mph, light trains have frequently run much faster. The express goods in the North Island are hauled by Da engines, and it was with great interest that I joined Da1463 at Paekakariki to sample diesel on a North Island Express Goods.

The train was a light 180 tons, as holiday goods traffic was sparse, 500 tons being the present maximum in normal traffic conditions. Despite being several minutes late out of Paekakariki the high-pitched whine of the generator in response to the notched-up controller soon had the traction motors turning rapidly, and after slowing for the crossover from double to single track, we blasted away at 50 towards Paraparaumu. The Da at this speed was a vastly different ride from a Ka on the same stretch of track. The engine was riding very smoothly and at 55 the air rushing past was louder than the sound of the motor, which was only a muffled rumble in the background as the Da – effortlessly it seemed – raced on with its light load. The Da has an 8-notch controller, and on flat track the movement of the lever into position 8 literally threw the train forward with a tremendous surge of power.

The Otaki Bank was surmounted with ludicrous ease as the throttle was notched back to keep her in check on the easy track past the grade. A great blast of sound reverberated all round as we passed under a ramp, the thunder of noise indicative of the brute strength of these engines. They may not be as fast as the Kas were, but for sheer pulling ability with a load of freight they have not been equalled by any previous New Zealand engine. Their power braking has been a big advantage on goods trains, enabling the train to be brought smoothly to a stop while the motor is still generating power. This keeps the couplings taut and has eliminated a lot of the crashing and jerking that often accompanied the stopping and starting of a long goods train.

At Levin we had our first stop, for some van traffic to be loaded, but were soon away again and thundering through Queen Street Station at 50 mph and on up the hill past the home of the old lady who waves to every train that passes. We took the grade at 50 with speed increasing until we crested the hill and cut the motor back to idle for the run down the other side. The dynamic brake was cut on and steadily reduced the speed of the train as it set up generation in the traction motors, slowing the whole train without the use of the normal brakes. Farms, fields, and hedges flashed by at near-express speeds as we headed towards Shannon over the easy flat countryside. The ride lacked the wild excitement of steam at speed, but it was fast running despite the deceptive lack of noise and bouncing deck. Seemingly only a coat of paint away from the cab roof, the Shannon Station verandah zipped past the clattering train.

We had been due to cross a southbound railcar at Shannon, but as we were running early and the car was running late, it was not until Longburn that we clattered over the points on to the loop to allow the car to pass while the rich smell of the Longburn Freezing Works forced its way into the cab. With the strength it had, there was no point in trying to keep it out, and we were relieved to open up and rumble out on to the main line again! Three miles and four minutes later we coasted to a halt at Palmerston North, having arrived, thanks to a lack of shunting at Otaki and light easy running, no less than 30 minutes early. We had in fact done the journey in a start-to-stop time of one hour and 29 minutes, a matter of minutes slower than most railcar schedules and two minutes less than the Limited is scheduled. For a goods train, even the Express Goods, it was pretty smart running, just on 45 mph average, stop to start. No wonder there had been one or two motorists on the way up whose jaws had dropped as a goods train overtook them!

For solid steady running at sustained speeds, the Da-hauled express goods trains are opening up new chapters in the history of freight haulage on the New Zealand Railways that augurs well for increased high-speed freights in the future. The Railways are getting the tools, and there can be no doubt that with them they are certainly doing the job.

Top: It's a hot day on the old Rimutaka Incline as four straining Fell engines inch their way towards the summit with a Wellington-bound goods. Only the gorse-covered hills now remain, but the Fells were much in evidence when this picture was taken (before October 1955).

Centre: This illustration shows two things: the superb view of the line from the cab of the Da class, and the construction problems that faced the builders of the Main Trunk. Here the line over the 238-foot high Makohine Viaduct disappears straight into a tunnel.

Bottom: Freshly painted, having just arrived from her Australian builders, with gleaming green bodywork and white trim, Di1100 being turned at Mason-ton after hauling a long test train on her maiden trip.

Top: Da1463, on which the author rode at the head of Train 630 express goods, is seen at Levin while parcels traffic is being loaded.

Centre: Dg788 was caught hauling a long stock train around the curve at Double Bridges north of Masterton on a fine day in the spring of 1960.

Bottom: Hauling an enthusiasts' excursion, Ab786 raises the echoes in a cutting as she charges along for the benefit of dozens of photographers. The line is the South Island's North Line a few miles south of Kaikoura.

10

Incidents and animals

IF THERE IS ONE CERTAINTY about any footplate trip, it is that there'll be no room for boredom. To the crew it may very well be a commonplace routine, but to the enthusiast it is the very stuff of life itself. There always seems to be some incident on every trip that adds a little touch of spice and variety. Such incidents sometimes give rise to humour, sometimes to discomfort, and sometimes to danger. Fortunately I have rarely, if ever, been exposed to the latter, but I've had my share of humour and discomfort.

On one occasion an Ab was steaming particularly poorly, which is unusual for this class. The fireman was reduced to raking the fire fairly frequently in order to get a good draught through the grate. Nothing seemed to be going right: it was a wet miserable day, the engine was slipping on the grades, and we were losing time all the way. The driver, with visions of a warm fireside awaiting him, was getting steadily more and more riled and began to argue that the raking was not doing any good. Finally he turned on his hapless mate, abused him roundly, seized the rake and tossed it out the cab!

His mate, who had been struggling to raise steam and growing more and more frustrated by the minute, was quick to respond. "All right! suit yourself then. B —— the bloody fire" – and promptly pitched the shovel out the side!

The two glared at each other momentarily, and then the driver slammed on the brakes and both men got out and retrieved the offending articles. There were some sheepish grins, and with honour apparently satisfied on both sides, the luckless crew set about getting their wretched engine home.

Wandering stock in these days of good fencing is less of a hazard than it was formerly, but the cow-catcher is still an essential part of even the latest diesel units. One memorable incident with a cow occurred on the Waitara line when I was on Ab748 taking

G

a load of wagons up to Lepperton. We were attacking the grade up to Lepperton with a full load of 220 tons when, as we staggered around a curve in a cutting, we saw an elderly cow grazing contentedly in the centre of the track.

The driver blew a shrieking blast on the whistle, old Daisy looked up at the black snorting monster bearing down on her, and contentedly resumed her meal.

In desperation the driver blew his whistle again; he couldn't afford to stop, for the old Ab would never have pulled away on the grade again. Inexorably closer we clattered and the cow disappeared from our vision obscured by the long boiler. We braced ourselves for the shock, as a cow has been known to derail the pilot truck of an Ab. We looked gingerly down from the cab expecting all manner of unsightly things to slide by beneath the churning drivers.

But suddenly, above the noise of the thrashing exhaust, could be heard the outraged bellowing of a highly disturbed farm animal. We looked forward and saw the rear of old Daisy cantering up the track ahead, her tail swishing indignantly from side to side. How she had turned and run in the split second since she had disappeared from view behind the smokebox we couldn't figure, but on a grade, as between a fully loaded Ab and a frightened cow, the latter gets my money every time.

On another occasion, a 60-total Da-powered goods was held up for several minutes by an even less imposing obstacle. We were waiting on a crossing loop (at Ohingaiti I think) for the northbound Daylight Limited to arrive when we first noticed a young lamb contentedly munching grass up nearer the crossover. A far-off Klaxon blared and an ever-approaching rumble announced the arrival of the Daylight, a Da and seven cars, which swept past us at an impressively high speed. The little white blob lunching down the tracks was obviously a steam enthusiast because this flurry of activity did not interfere with his meal. Ahead of us, the CTC light turned to green and we rumbled slowly down the loop to the crossover. As we had anticipated, one who had taken no notice of the Daylight could hardly be expected to take note of a humble freight. Several reverberating Klaxon blasts failed to make him move. As we slowed, the fireman glanced at his watch and remarked, "Oh well, it's only 11.29, we're not really due to leave for another minute anyway, according to the timetable."

We stopped a few feet from the placidly munching lamb and the fireman made ready to jump down and remove the woolly trespasser. At that moment it looked up, paused, leapt nimbly from the track and scuttled off. We all glanced at our watches, it was exactly 11.30. As we looked at the disappearing lamb we could have sworn he had a working timetable clutched under one hoof.

Despite its appearance, the steam locomotive is a relatively simple piece of machinery, which accounts for its great reliability. From time to time things do go wrong with even the best ordered machine and the results may be serious or perhaps merely annoying. In the former category was an experience I had on a Jb on the Stratford-Taumaranui line when north of Ohura we noticed that the engine had began to run roughly. It soon became obvious that something was wrong so we stopped, miles from anywhere in the bush at the back of beyond, and investigated. The trouble was eventually traced to the lubricator. This useful and important item of equipment provides the lubricating oil that ensures the pistons move freely; if it packs up, the eventual result is overheating, and then seizure, effectively stalling the engine completely.

It was not at first apparent what was wrong, and the crew proceeded to remove impressively large bolts from the lubricator to investigate. The problem was acute, because to try and proceed to Taumaranui was to risk doing serious damage to the engine and possibly seizing it completely, while it was obviously going to be a long wet walk to any train control phone and an even longer wait for a relief engine. We spent some anxious moments until the trouble was traced, but fortunately repairs could be effected and somewhat gingerly, we steamed off again. The repairs held, and it was with a good deal of relief that we finally crept into Taumaranui and the welcome sanctuary of the engine sheds.

A merely annoying fault was experienced on a Kb on the long drag up to Arthur's Pass when the steam cock on the booster unit was stuck. The booster is located on the rear axle of the trailing truck and is designed for extra tractive effort at low speeds. The unit was not engaged, but we spent the whole trip enveloped in swirling steam that blew up through the connecting plates and around the cab entrances. A Kb is a mighty steamer and we were uncomfortably hot and wet by the time Arthur's Pass was reached. It can be fairly cool at the Pass; and arriving there after a long term steam-bath was mighty unpleasant when we exchanged the warm damp atmosphere of the cab for the cold bracing night air.

Another wetting experience, but of a rather warmer nature, occurred on a Ka on the Main Trunk as we were nearing the southern portal of the Mangaweka Tunnel. Suddenly the water-level-gauge glass shattered and for some unknown reason the ball which stops the water flow in such event failed to seat. At that precise moment, we plunged into the tunnel. It was a nightmare. Hot water and steam were sprayed all around the cab. It was too late to stop and reverse out, all that could be done was to open the regulator and hope for daylight before we were scalded or soaked completely. We roared out of the Tunnel, the cab a haze of steam and hot water, and ground to a halt, where repairs were made and the gauge shut off. The whole episode had taken only minutes, but they were exceptionally uncomfortable ones. Engine crews have long struggled for decent facilities and clean working conditions, but ready-made hot shower facilities provided on the footplate itself somehow did not particularly impress the unfortunate crew as a desirable locomotive amenity!

The number of people who will have trains on at level crossings is surprising, and several engines I have been travelling on have narrowly missed colliding with foolish individuals who think they can beat the train. Crews get quite upset about this, not so much in anger, as just plain fright lest they might hit the idiot motorist. A Ka, at 145 tons, or a Da at 78 tons and travelling only at 30 mph is a fairly solid object to be hit by, as some motorists obviously fail to realise. Combined bridges, which fortunately are now rapidly disappearing, are another source of potential danger, and it was on one of these that I once noticed the terrific acceleration of which a Mini-Minor can be capable. North of Reefton one day in a Vulcan railcar we approached a combined bridge which has fairly poor visibility. We had slowed to the required 6 mph, when out of nowhere a Mini drove on to the bridge, heading the same way as we were. The railcar driver stamped on the horn at about the same moment that the driver of the Mini happened to look in his rear vision mirror. What his thoughts were as he saw a railcar heading for his tail I don't know, but from the rubber that was left on the bridge decking I can well imagine! It was hardly any exaggeration to say he was flying when he bounced off the end of that bridge at full acceleration.

Nowadays, with frequent track inspection and better rails, derailments due to faults in the track are less frequent than they once were. I had one experience of near-derailment at Hokitika one day when returning to Greymouth on the afternoon mixed from Ross. We were travelling very slowly on the loop, ready to stop, when we felt the engine pull slightly, and at the same instant a shunter, galvanised into motion, came running towards us. It didn't need me to tell the crew that something was wrong; the driver slammed on the emergency brake and we shuddered to a halt.

We dropped down from the engine and ran back to where the shunter was standing looking very perplexedly at the ground. We soon saw the trouble. Under the weight of a heavily loaded Lc wagon a piece of rail about 2 feet long had broken and, still upright, had apparently sunk into the ballast of clay, shingle, oil and muck, leaving a drop of almost 4 inches along the gap. It was a ticklish situation; the gap could very easily tip the wagon completely, for it was neatly straddling the gap, one axle on either side of it. It was undoubtedly only our crawling speed that had prevented this before.

The gap was too great for the engine to negotiate safely, as the drivers would probably have failed to climb the break, so reversing off the loop was obviously out. The only thing to do seemed to be to split the train and hope that the heavily laden, high gravity centred wagon would stay upright. We uncoupled the train at the van end of the offending wagon and went back to the engine. The driver eased off the brakes and with the reverse lever right forward, opened the regulator a notch. We inched forward and all eyes turned to the wagon. Suddenly it canted at a seemingly impossible angle apparently headed for a certain wheels-over-tarpaulin act. Just as suddenly, the driving-wheels began to spin and the driver hurriedly slammed on the brakes and shut off steam.

It was quite obvious what had happened: the wagon wheel had caught on the near edge of the rail and stuck. Slowly and steadily was certainly not going to solve this one. The only solution was obviously to give the engine her head, and drag the wagon up by brute force, praying that it wouldn't tip. Again the brakes were eased off, and simultaneously the sander and regulator were opened. The Ab bucked like a mustang as the wheels spun, caught, then gripped and moved forward. The wagon lurched over drunkenly and then miraculously it bumped up on to good track and part of the problem was over. It now remained to collect the back half of our train, shunt and reassemble it, all without the use of the main loop. We eventually succeeded and whistled out of Hokitika leaving a worried shunter wondering how he was going to cross and shunt two goods trains that night whose total was about twice the loop space that he had available. But that was his problem. . . .

One journey I made on the West Coast will long live in my memory as the nearest thing to a sample of Dante's Inferno that I ever wish to meet. It was delightful summer day in Greymouth in January 1966 when I joined the crew of J1216 that was to take a summer holiday express as far as Otira on its run to Christchurch. It was already hot outside, and it was hotter still on the footplate of the J where a carefully banked fire licked hungrily at the coals and roared up over the arch.

The engine was in good form and the run through to Stillwater along the banks of the Grey River, glistening below in the sunshine, was a pleasant one, as the exhaust roared away and the J rattled merrily along with a 6-total train. Soon the track began the long climb that would lead eventually to the mountains at Otira and the rhythm of the fireman's work with the shovel increased. The J class at the best of times are very warm engines, and today was no exception. Cicadas crackled in the trees and the heat shimmered off the roadbed as we began labouring up towards the small whistle stop of Jackson.

The Js have air-operated fire doors which are activated by the fireman stamping on a pedal on the floor of the cab as he swings round with his shovelful of coal; the doors are in two halves which swing apart to allow the coal to be flung into the inferno within the firebox. The climb up to Otira is a long hard one: from Jackson, the grade averages 1 in 66 for the 11 long miles up to Otira, and it is heavy going for any engine. The fireman's only hope is to build and then maintain the hottest fire he can to make sure of the best possible reading on his enemy the pressure gauge.

As we approached Jackson, the fire doors gave their first indication of trouble. The fireman, whose name was George, swung round with his full load of coal, tramped on the pedal and swung. There was a loud clang, the coal flew all over the cab and the fire doors remained obstinately shut. George cursed fluently, as much from the jar of the shovel striking the doors as from the provocation of the action. A test tramp on the pedal swung the doors open perfectly however, and George again commenced his easy, swinging, firing rhythm. On the last swing however, the doors stayed open. A quick belt with the shovel and they met shut with a resounding clang, but the beginnings of trouble were apparent.

We roared through Jackson with the cut-off shortened and the regulator wide out as the J was made ready for the struggle ahead. George took up his shovel, glanced with some apprehension at his mate and the doors, and commenced firing. The doors banged open and the coal disappeared; the doors hung obstinately open. The fireman stamped the pedal, the right-hand door moved slightly but the left one not at all. There was some more fluent cursing and the offending door was repeatedly belted with the shovel. It was all to no avail.

A large piece of piping was the next weapon selected from the footplate armoury and both driver and fireman attacked the offending door with zest. Mighty blows rained down, and had any of them missed, half of the fireman's controls would have been shattered. In the excitement it was realised that we were pounding along at a steady 35 mph up the grade without any lookout being kept. The driver gave one last despairing bang, shouted "Leave the bastard", flung himself into his seat and peered quickly ahead.

Meanwhile, the steam pressure gauge had been slipping rapidly down and was now hovering on the 175-lb reading. The fireman grabbed his shovel and once more set to heaving coal into the fire.

I have said that the footplate of a J is hot. At this particular time on this particular engine on this particular piece of steep track, that remark would have qualified as the understatement of the year. The heat grew worse; it now seemed like a malignant force bound to melt us all. The driver leaned further out of his window and drew his legs away from the awful heat pouring from the almost white-hot maw of the firebox.

The steam pressure was rising now but so was the heat. From 6 feet away, the cab behind the driver's seat was too hot for me to hang on to any more. I got some relief by standing in the cab entrance and hanging on to the window-frame, but it was still insufferably hot. Inside, George, sweat-soaked and beet-red, the sweat running off his face and dropping on to his shovel, alone faced the onslaught of heat. Firing's heavy work at the best of times, but in that cab it must have been quite intolerable. By this time I was grasping the handrails and hanging backwards out of the cab as we forged steadily up the grades and round the curves and I looked longingly at the cool, fresh water of the mountain streams beside which we were running.

Suddenly, up ahead, nestled below the line of the mountains, snowcapped even in January, could be seen Otira. The J now had sufficient steam to cope by herself and with a final curse George threw down his shovel and imitated me by hanging out of the opposite side of the cab as we chuffed into Otira where the electrics were waiting for us. We uncoupled, and steamed off down to loco where, to everyone's intense relief, an offending bolt which had caught on the backhead was removed.

That trip was possibly the only time in my life that I have ever wished that we had a diesel on the head end.

11

Wooden cars through the backblocks

BY PRACTICAL DEFINITION, the mixed train was a blob of smoke on the horizon that slowly resolved into a steam locomotive, often of the older variety, a usually short string of goods wagons and, bumping along in the rear just ahead of or sometimes behind the guard's van, a generally decrepit old wooden carriage. With open platforms, dirty smoke-blackened exterior and the faded, cracked, leather seats of its old car, the ever-diminishing mixed train, a form of transport almost as old as the steam locomotive itself, clanked slowly and sedately past on its leisurely journey. Despite its age, the mixed train, unlike its steam locomotive contemporary in the North Island, has survived into the diesel age albeit, to many, in an emasculated form.

In the days when private cars were few and tarsealed roads even more rare, the mixed train held undisputed sway as the means of communal transport. When towns and rural settlements were linked by the steel ribbons or sprang up in their wake, there followed as a natural consequence, like thunder after lightning, the little mixed train. The slow, fussy little train that so frequently was the only reliable means of day-to-day communication with the world that waited just round the bend where the shining ribbons disappeared into the distances beyond. Children travelled to school, farmers to market, housewives to shop in the nearest large settlement, families to visit, people of all types with all their varied reasons for travel – all knew this train in an age where time was still a servant and the ulcer mere indigestion.

Time and social conditions have sounded the death knell of the mixed train. In some places the bell still tolls, though so faintly as to be virtually inaudible; in others the last notes have died away, and with them, so many of these diminutive mixed trains. Once hardly a stretch of track in the country lacked its (usually) daily mixed train. Now they are increasingly few and far between, and some still listed in the timetables have in fact disappeared. The "picture trains" that ran on Saturday nights to the nearest large towns were once packed with cheerful families out for a night on the town and fun with the Marx Brothers or excitement with Bill Boyd, before the train carried them back again into the bush and the backblocks.

Today only one remnant of the picture train survives in the North Island. It is Mixed Train 434, Taumarunui to Te Kuiti, and the return Train 437 which runs only on Saturdays, although 434 is a daily (Monday-Saturday) train. The old Ohakune picture trains which ran south from Taumarunui and north from Taihape have finally succumbed in this age of television and the private car. On the day I slung my bag into the old battered carriage, Train 434 was a long diesel-hauled goods train, on to which, like some afterthought on the part of the shunter, was tacked the passenger service. I was the sole occupant of the car, dimly lit in late afternoon sunlight, when the diesel at the head gathered momentum out over the crossovers of the Taumarunui yards. The odd cigarette butt lay abandoned on the pitted lino floor, but otherwise the car was clean and, in a spartan, horsehair-padding fashion, tolerably comfortable. The Department quite correctly advertise that the railway is a great way of seeing the countryside while someone else worries about the driving. They do not mention though what every enthusiast knows: the *best* way of all to see the scenery is from the earliest type of observation-car – the rear platform of an old carriage rambling along at the tail-end of a mixed train.

The railway runs north of Taumarunui along the banks of the Ongarue River, where leafy green willows dip in the breeze and dangle in the cool water of the river as the bushclad hills retreat into the distance. North of Ongarue, where once the laboured gasping of the little Heisler bush engine could be heard, rocky slopes loom grey and precipitous. The shattered rock is partially covered in scrub and secondary growth. A mass of pines rear their trunks to the sky on a rocky bluff over the river, and the Canadian-built Da must feel at home as its pulsating roar sounds out over the river and echoes back off the cliff face. The several solid rock outcrops through which the line cuts are eloquent testimony to the sweating labour of the bearded navvies with their picks, shovels, and barrows that forced the line through this scenic wilderness.

The wild ruggedness gives way again to farmlands north of Waimaki as the train starts the long slog up to the Porootarao Tunnel. This was completed in 1890, 10 years before the rails reached the township of the same name and 13 years before it was in regular use. The Tunnel gave considerable difficulty in access to the contractors, and it was found necessary to build a brick kiln on the site to avoid having to pack the bricks in for the lining. In the centre of the Tunnel, 1,148 feet above sea level, is the crest of a ridge, the highest point on the line between Taumarunui and Te Kuiti. As the train enters the Tunnel the entrance becomes even smaller, but the orange-coloured disc with the flattened bottom, rather like a moon in the inky blackness of space suddenly begins to set, and it is an uncanny sensation to watch the disc drop below the "horizon" as the train picks up speed on the down-grade out of the tunnel.

At Mangapehi is a timber mill, and here two old bush loco-motives, both geared engines of American manufacture – a Climax and a Heisler – lie on a siding undergoing repairs that will even-tually see them operating again under the tender care of a dedi-cated group of enthusiasts. Train 434 was running ahead of time and sat with the engine throbbing gently on the main track await-ing clearance. In better days, several passengers would have boarded the train here for a night at the Te Kuiti pictures, but when the signal changed to green I was still the sole passenger and remained so until in the gathering twilight the train entered Te Kuiti. Like so many others of the mixed trains that once provided a virtual through service on the Main Trunk (if one had several days to spare) Train 434 must soon vanish from the pages of the timetable into the legion of the lost.

A surprising number of mixed trains still survive in the North Island. The Northland line still sees mixed trains to Henderson, and to Opua, while others make the long slow plod from Frankton to Rotorua through the bush around Mamaku and the pumice lands of the plateau. But in the North Island, for my money, the Stratford mixed trains still best symbolise those of that bygone era when the wooden cars trundled along through the bush.

The Stratford line is probably less known than any other trunk line in the country. The passenger on the Taranaki line sees it as a track running away to the left as he heads south from Stratford in a railcar. The Main Trunk passenger will see it only from the Daylight Limited, shortly after it pulls out of Taumarunui on its spectacular run north. In between these two points runs the Strat-ford-Okahukura line, meandering its way through the backblocks of Taranaki and the King Country. The only passengers who ever see this line travel on the mixed trains that wander through, or on an enthusiasts' excursion. All other services, railcars and relief expresses, pass through during the night hours. This is a great pity, because the line is scenically beautiful with its mixture of pasture and towering bushclad hills.

My introduction to the Stratford line was from the cab of Jb1205, one of the roughest riding steamers I've ever been on. Her compensating gear was shot and the back springs might just as well not have been fitted. She thumped rather than rode the rails, in a bonejarring series of crashes from one rail joint to the other. The noise in the cab was tremendous, like a pile driver hammering bridge piles. For all her bad riding however she was a game old girl, her exhaust beat was a staccato series of explosions that literally shook soot from the roof of some of the tunnels, and her acceleration away from stops was a joy to experience.

Less of a joy though was riding her in the tunnels. Belching smoke eddied and swirled all around the side of the engine. Choking fumes poured into the cab as the exhaust thundered in the narrow space and more smoke poured from the stack. My lungs literally clogged, I gasped and wheezed and stuffed a handkerchief further into my mouth as in the confines of the Okahu Tunnel Jb1205 really poured it on. The almost one-mile length of the Tunnel finally came to an end and, gagging and coughing, we hit the fresh air outside. In the words of the gasping driver, "We damn near qualify for a miner's pension on this line." The Okahu Tunnel is the final one in a gauntlet of 24 that crews on the Stratford line had to run in steam days.

Steam on the Stratford line is now unhappily a thing of the past. No longer do crews choke in the Okahu Tunnel, and the Js lie rusting on the rip tracks. Their place has been taken by the ever-increasing Da class which now handle all trains on the line. The fascination of steam may have gone but the inherent fascination and visual splendour of the line itself still remains, in no way diminished by the less spectacular motive power now employed.

The best way of seeing the Stratford line is to take Train 555, the 9 a.m. mixed train out of Stratford, for a leisurely plod through to Taumarunui. A sunny morning with scuds of cloud blowing over from Mt Egmont was the scene at the Stratford Station one Saturday morning when I arrived to sample mixed train travel on the Stratford line. It had been a fascinating trip on the Jb, but a steam engine cab with all its noise and soot and heat and vibration is not the best place from which to see the scenery. Train 555 was the archetype of all mixed trains: three open wagons, a cattle wagon, the car and the van, were the sole make-up of the train, the old wooden car symbolic of mixed trains everywhere. Only the throbbing bulk of Da1462 betrayed the fact that this was not some scene set back to 40 years before.

The Stratford yards were busy, A Dsb shunter clattered to and fro amid the crashing of couplings and the squeal of brakeblocks, while several long goods trains stood on the loop tracks, and a Da growled slowly past on her way to the head of a New Plymouth-bound goods train.

I was the only occupant of the car as the signal changed, the great 12-cylinder motor roared up to a crescendo of vibrating noise, and we moved slowly off as the Stratford Post Office clock struck the hour. We clattered around the bend behind the loco shed and off through the rolling green fields towards Toko. The diminutive train, clattering and banging, bounced along behind the bulk of the locomotive, grossly and ludicrously overpowered for such a load, the mere 100 tons making absolutely no difference to her performance. We were off on the first miles of a line that has many features absolutely unique to it.

The idea of a railway east from Stratford dates back to 1880, when a line from Stratford to Te Awamutu via Tangarakau was proposed as one possible route for the Main Trunk. Surveys were made from Stratford in 1880, 1887, and 1888, but not until 1897 did concrete proposals come about when it was suggested that the Stratford County Council construct a tramway. Nothing came of this, but Taranaki at last got its railway from Stratford when the first train ran to Toko in June 1902, after construction had begun in March the previous year. The progress of the railway to Toko and Douglas (11 miles) was marked by sawmilling and intensive farming. It was through this farmland that Da1462 was hauling her train at a steady 35 mph. The country is green and rolling, lush and beautiful, and the line undulates gently as it curves around through the paddocks. The line when seen from the footplate is like a gentle roller-coaster going up and down in a succession of little grades and dips.

North of Toko lay great lengths of welded rail, and the mixed clanked slowly over the track that would shortly be torn up. Much of the track was replaced at the time the Das took over the running, as their greater capacity meant longer trains and faster running on the more difficult sections. We clattered without pause through Douglas and on past the old brickworks whose tall cracked chimney rears precariously up above the kilns built back into the hillside, the mouth of the kiln looking like the tunnels of some miniature railway. Past Douglas, the hilly nature of the country that was to persist for the rest of the run became apparent.

The Da's snarl echoed off the sides of the first major cutting as the line entered the first ridge of hills and wound along them on an upgrade. From here on, the country began to reflect the character of the Taranaki inland that made the construction of the line such a monumental work.

Perhaps nowhere else in New Zealand was such a combination of climatic and topographical disadvantages encountered in such intensity. The uplifted marine deposits of mudstone and massive sandstone have been deeply eroded by meandering rivers. Although the hills are not particularly high, only 600-700 feet, the rivers have cut down so much in some places that it may be 1,000 feet from the river bottom to the crest of the ridges. These features are responsible for the many bridges and culverts on the line, the construction of which was considerably hampered by the high rainfall, averaging 73 inches per annum. Much of the rainfall in this area is in the form of thunderstorms and these gave the builders of the line considerable trouble by sweeping away bridges and embankments.

The line progresses through a series of picturesque little valleys and just past the 19-mile peg at Kiore cuts through the first tunnelled ridge. As we approached Te Wera the brakes hissed on and we rumbled to our first stop. No one got on and a minute later the motor revved up again and we clanked off. From the surprised look on the face of the guard as he poked his head around the door, it was obvious that passengers were an infrequent occurrence on the train and normally the once-a-week shopping expedition to town is the only time that human freight is carried to any great extent. The line ran on up towards the Pohukura saddle and the train plunged for the second time into the heart of the ridges. The third tunnel has a feature common to many on the line; it is curved in an S shape and the wide Da throttled back considerably as the narrow walls swept past.

Out in the sunshine again I stood on the front platform of the swaying carriage. The pleasure of standing out on the bouncing platform of a wooden car as it rattles and bumps along, the wind tearing through one's hair and battering one's eyes, feet stationed firmly and bending in time to the jerking rhythm – this is the pleasure that only mixed trains with wooden cars can give. The simple pleasure of banging up the window and hanging out in the breeze as the train sweeps around the curve is something no first-class car can ever offer.

We had no further stops on the run through to Whangamomona, as there was no shunting and no passengers to pick up. We arrived at Whangamomona almost an hour ahead of schedule and had to wait for the westbound mixed to arrive. Whanga is a little township nestling in the heart of the bush and hills, with a store that sells everything from groceries, to jeans, to TV sets, and a post office, a garage, and a pleasant little hostelry where the reigning Maori darts champion beat me for a round of Taranaki's best bitter.

The westbound mixed duly rumbled in, a long train of heavily-loaded wagons, and the two trains sat looking at each other for half an hour to enable some small children off the westbound train to get the family milk supply from the store before joining the Taumarunui-bound train to go back up the line home. These little girls and a woman heavily laden with groceries were indicative of the vital function the railways once played as a social influence, when the only way to get to town was on the mixed train, when the railway was one of the most important social assets to any community.

Leaving Whanga at 11.35 we travelled on further into the backblocks farmlands, until at Tahora we stopped for our first shunt, dropping off an empty Lc wagon on a weed-grown siding. Tahora was for many years the terminus of the line from Stratford. The going had become steadily more difficult as the line was pushed on from Douglas. Whangamomona was reached in July 1914, when the First World War greatly retarded tracklaying. After the War work resumed on an easy basis, the line being built in one section while the next was being surveyed, until in November 1924 the rails reached the little bush clearing that was Tahora. It had taken a quarter of a century for the 47 miles to be pushed that far. Ahead lay the formidable barrier between the Tangarakau and Heao Rivers.

Construction from the eastern end had begun in 1911. A last-minute decision to change the junction from Ongarue to Okahukura, six miles south, saved the Railways Department six miles of line and $120,000, but it failed the land speculators who had hoped to make a profit on land at Ongarue. The great stumbling block to construction was the 74 chains of the Okahukura Tunnel which had to be driven before work could really advance any further into the Ohura Valley. A service road was formed, the contracts let and 130 men started work in January 1914.

The Tunnel was difficult to construct and has been a constant source of trouble ever since. A year after starting, the contractor went bankrupt, the papa, many watercourses and continual wet weather proved just too much for him. Another contractor tried, in 1917 he failed, and the Government took over the work. Even then, the Tunnel was not completed until 1921, at which point the formation work on the line had reached Matiere, 10 miles away. Flooding has always been a problem: shortly before the line opened, a flash-flood choked the whole length of the Okahu Tunnel with logs and mud, and it took weeks to clear it out. The Railways Department has recently constructed a major flood diversion race at the eastern end of the Tunnel to prevent water backing up into it, and at long last it may be that No. 24 tunnel, smoke no longer a problem to crews, may cease to be a problem to track gangs and engineers.

Leaving Tahora our mixed train began the most spectacular part of its run, through the bush and tunnels of the Tangarakau section. There are some beautiful scenic spots as the railway enters the bush proper; the line curves along through thick bush, lichens and creepers festoon the trees, and water drips off the branches into the damp undergrowth following a drizzle or shower. The bellow of the engine cracks out over the noise of the rumbling wheels of the train as the line curves up through the bush, and the train plunges into several short tunnels before coming out into the little valley that is Tangarakau.

To traverse the core of difficult country that separated the two railheads in 1928, no less than six tunnels were built in a distance of eight miles. The tunnelling was retarded considerably by erosion at the portals, and brick lining was essential to stop the soft papa from caving in on the workmen beneath. Extensive preparations had been made in 1926 and 1927 for the assault. The two prime necessities before work could commence were access and accommodation. A feature of the construction from both ends was the great use made of service tramways. A four-and-a-half-mile line was laid to the first tunnel and jig lines were rigged over the ridges to allow materials to be sent from one side to the other. What was, at the time, the largest public works camp in the country was erected, and the standard of facilities was a vast improvement on the primitive conditions that had previously obtained in such camps.

A powerhouse using local coal was erected, and several 2 foot 6 inch gauge electric locomotives used for the Otira Tunnel construction were brought in to assist in the work. Ballast had to be railed in from as far away as Mt Egmont and this further increased the cost. Trams, trucks, horses, men and sledges were all used to try to speed the work, made so slow and costly by the unique combination of physical difficulties. This final eight-mile section ultimately cost $700,000 and was one of the most expensive sections of track anywhere in the country. Fittingly, this was the only railway work not suspended during the Depression and perseverance had its reward when the completed section was finally handed over to the Railways Department in September 1934.

At Tangarakau the train stopped while the guard rang in to Train Control, and there was several minutes' pause in which to stand and savour what it must have been like to have lived for several years in this part of the country, lacking in all amenities except Nature itself which, beautiful as it is, must have palled after five winters in the rain and slush of the construction camp.

At the invitation of the guard I joined him at Tangarakau for coffee in his cubbyhole at the rear of the van. Few members of the public appreciate the conditions some of the guards are forced to work under. The woodwork in the compartment was cracked and peeling, and one of the racks of pigeonholes for papers hung drunkenly from the wall of the van, which must have been well over 60 years old. In the tunnels, the feeble yellow light of an archaic oil lamp illuminated the guard's reports and consignment notes, provided that they were held no further than 2 feet away from the wick.

The surroundings were grim but the company pleasant, and we yarned away for many pleasant miles as the train ground its way further on towards Ohura, through the bush and papa banks. Many of the stations on the line are on curves, or straights so short that around the bend at each end are notices to inform the driver how many wagon lengths he is from the main points for shunting purposes. It is no good expecting to get directions from the guard or station agent, who will be well hidden behind a bluff around the station curve.

At Heao, 59 miles out, we dropped off our cattle wagon and so elevated the train almost to passenger status, as the only goods wagons now remaining were two empty Lc open wagons. It was even less trouble then for the Da to maintain the authorised 35 mph and we rocked and bounced along in the little 11-ton van, which was considerably less comfortable at this speed than even old Jb1205 had been on the same stretch of track. There were no coal wagons to be picked up from the mine at Mangaparo, though the bucket rigs normally bring in about 16 wagonloads a day over the ridges from the opencast mine to the loading bins.

We drew into Ohura for a further wait of an hour before it was time to pull out again, such had been our steady shuntless rate of progress. Saturday is a fairly uneventful day on the branch; there is little traffic, and most Taumarunui-bound trains consist of

Jb1205 is spick and span, brass plates gleaming in wintry sunshine as she prepares to leave Stratford with an enthusiasts' excursion for Taumarunui. The Jb is the oilburning conversion of the 1939 J class engines.

Left: Rumbling quietly away to itself at the head of the Stratford-Taumarunui Mixed Train sits Da1462. Even with a diesel the charm of Mixed Train travel remains.

Right: There's no laborious shovelling of coal into buckets at Greymouth. Ab823 is getting a full bunker in the space of a few minutes at the Greymouth coaling tower.

Top: One of the 1,800 hp Ew class electrics glides silently out of Paeka-kariki with a local train for Wellington in tow.

Centre: Being brought out of their stall at Otira, ready to haul an east-bound express through the Otira Tunnel to Arthurs Pass, are three Eo class electrics, now over "forty years on".

Bottom: The magnificent eighteen-stall roundhouse at Greymouth, a sight unique in New Zealand. Two Js, a Wf, and an Ab are enjoying the sun outside their stalls. Only Invercargill and Lyttelton had other examples of this traditionally-American steam locomotive structure.

empties. About twice as much freight comes in from Taumarunui as goes out from Stratford, and such diversions as an hour's eeling before it is time to depart are not unknown.

It is difficult to avoid the conclusion that economically the line is hard to justify. The railway did not stimulate the development in the back country that had been hoped for, and settlers were leaving the district even after the railway had been completed. Very little traffic is generated over the line, most trains consisting of through tonnage to or from the more inhabited areas of Taranaki. In 1930 the Railways Board stated that: "The operation of this line will result in a heavy loss without any apparent increase in revenue, unless by the development of the coal mine at Tangarakau."

Even with the Government's decision in 1932 not to construct trunk roads in the area, the railway was too late to pick up the cream of much of the traffic that was being conveyed by the coast road from Te Kuiti to New Plymouth. Nevertheless, the line has been important as an alternative route, as I found when instead of travelling on 221, the Auckland-Wellington Saturday Night Express, down the Main Trunk, I finished up journeying back over the line that same night, because two goods trains had derailed and blocked the main line near Ohakune, diverting the express through Taranaki.

Train 555 however was not concerned with whether the tracks it was clicking along on were economical or not, and the miles slipped by and the afternoon wore on as in the snug interior of the rattling van with its smoky little stove, my guard friend and I chatted while the countryside slipped past the bay windows. A hollow rumble told us we were crossing the twin-deck road-rail bridge over the Ongarue River; the wheels crashed over the loop points as we drew into Okahukura Station, waited for the CTC light to change, and headed off down the trunk for the short run to Taumarunui, six miles away.

In a light misty rain so typical of the township, the Da eased her little train shamefacedly past two other Das waiting to move out with great long train loads of tonnage, and appropriately we were relegated to one of the very outer loops. I said farewell to my friend the guard, and swung down from the rough-riding little van. Train 555 and I had arrived at Taumarunui on a split-second timing that would have made the Limited blush.

For how much longer the old wooden cars of the daily mixed

trains will run is not certain. It cannot be for very much longer, but while they do, the Stratford line with its bush, tunnels, valleys, and old wooden cars beckons the enthusiast. To anyone with an eye for natural beauty, a nostalgia for the days of windblown hair, creaking wood, and windows that really open up, then the Stratford line, diesels notwithstanding, is a passport to the good old days, when railway travel was an adventure rather than a mere means of transportation.

12

On the Midland Line

THE ONLY RAILWAY IN THE COUNTRY that runs east-west from coast to coast in a direct line is the South Island's Midland Line from Rolleston to Greymouth by way of Springfield, Arthur's Pass, Otira, and Stillwater. The line climbs from sea level to 2,433 feet to sea level again, through rich coastal plains and past rugged crags, mountains, and bush, and it is the vital link between the great natural resources of the West Coast and the factories and farms of the east. In its length it probably offers more contrast in scenery, climate, and land development than any other similar length of track in New Zealand. In many ways it is unique, and its long and at times tumultuous history dates back to the early days of the Colony, when men of vision looked to the day when a railway might tap the wealth of Westland.

The first agitation for an east-west railway came from the province of Nelson, then territorially a much vaster area than today, comprising a considerable portion of the West Coast down as far as Greymouth as well as the counties of Cheviot and Amuri. Because the province proposed to find the finance itself there was little opposition to the passing of the Nelson and Cobden Railway Acts of 1866-1869. These Acts covered the first sections of a proposal to build a railway running from Foxhill, then the terminus of the Nelson line, down through the Buller Gorge, bypass Reefton (to be served by a branch line) and on to Cobden on the north bank of the Grey River mouth. From there the line was to cross the Southern Alps and link up with the Amuri county of the Nelson Province.

It is interesting to speculate on the chances of this ambitious project had the Provincial Governments stayed in office. Work might well have speedily been put in hand, but its ultimate completion by a province seems more doubtful. The Public Works Policy of 1870 committed the Government to main trunk railways in both Islands, and not risking their venture in case they did not so qualify, Nelson set about investigating a company to build the line by private enterprise. At this point the Central Government stepped in, and undertook, if the company project was abandoned, "to bring Nelson and the West Coast into communication with Canterbury, and also, if it should be found expedient, into communication with Marlborough". The Railways Act of 1873 authorised the construction of the Nelson and East Coast links. With the passing of the provinces however, and the looming depression, the line proceeded no further than its statutory authority.

Meanwhile, in Canterbury, agitation had been developing, concentrated naturally on the east-west link rather than the complementary Nelson section. Throughout 1878 Canterbury meetings called for the construction of a line as an extension of the existing line through Amberley. There was a real fear at the time that Otago would win the day with a proposal for a railway through the Haast Pass. Had Canterbury known how long it was to be before even a road went through the Haast Pass, their agitation might not have been as brisk. The Public Works Statement of 1878 was a bold one. Among other things it proposed two routes to Brunnerton, both of which were to be constructed, the one via Amberley and the other via Otago Central. Canterbury's hopes were dashed however when the Government was defeated the following year and the great scheme crashed with it.

In 1880 meetings were held in Canterbury with a view to forming a company to finance and construct an east-west link, but the three commissioners asked to investigate the proposal came to the conclusion that the line could not possibly prove remunerative to the shareholders. The proposal in 1882 by the Government to build a Hurunui-Picton line — which no one at that stage was interested in — added insult to injury. The following year the East and West Coast Railway League was formed to press for the Midland Line. An extremely comprehensive report by a commission of five headed by Capt. W. R. Russell made extensive on-the-spot investigations of no less than 11 routes, but again the verdict was disappointing and the cost of $3,600,000, for a line via Arthur's Pass, was not recommended. The vital problem, that of routes, had however been solved, and the commission was unanimously in favour of Arthur's Pass.

The final steps towards formation of the Midland Railway Company can be traced from Sir Julius Vogel's Act of 1884 authorising the construction of a line from Springfield via Arthur's Pass, to be built by a syndicate. A contract was signed for the construction of the line on 17 January 1885, and the same day Arthur Dobson and two others sailed for London. In London an offer was received from the American firm of Meiggs & Company to construct the line at a cost of $7,720,000, but this was considered too costly and the proposal was defeated when it came before Parliament for approval. The demonstrations and agitation proceeded anew.

Finally however came the reward. On 15 March 1886 negotiations were completed with a syndicate in London to float the New Zealand Midland Railway Company, with a capital of $1,000,000 in $20 shares, and on 19 April the Company was registered. Its history however was destined to be unfortunate.

On 3 August 1888 the Company contracted with the Crown for the construction of a railway to connect at Springfield and Brunnerton with existing Government lines and to go from Brunnerton via Reefton to connect with the Nelson Railway at Belgrove. The contract was made pursuant to the Midland Railway Contract Act, 1887. This Contract (Clause 2) provided that: "The company shall and will with all convenient speed and within the term of ten years computed from the 17th day of January 1885 . . . construct and completely finish a line of railway" [from Springfield to Brunnerton to Belgrove].

The earlier Act, the East and West Coast (Middle Island) and Nelson Railway and Railways Construction Act 1884, had as its object the completion of a railway which together with the existing lines would form a trunk line through the South Island from Nelson to the Bluff, and would unite Nelson and Westland with the East Coast. The Midland Railway Company was formed for the purpose of constructing these lines, and under its enabling Act of 1887 received the go-ahead for its mammoth task.

Besides construction of the actual railway lines, the line was to be "maintained and worked . . . with all necessary buildings, works, and appliances requisite for working the same". The estimated cost of construction was $5,000,000, and the Company was entitled to Crown land grants equal to 50 per cent of the cost of work completed. To assess this figure the line was divided into 35 sections from Springfield to Belgrove, and on completion of a section the land was to be handed over by the Crown in accordance with the contract.

The Company began work in 1887 and by 1894 had constructed lines from Brunnerton to Reefton and Brunnerton to Jacksons, forming a complete line from Jacksons to Reefton. This however was only a total length of constructed line of 75 miles out of the 235 provided for by the contract. Moreover it was by far the easiest and least expensive portion. Ahead in one direction lay the massive barrier of the Southern Alps; in the other the crag and bush of the Upper Buller Gorge and the wild country around Murchison.

Early in 1894, beset by difficulties, the Company ceased construction, having completed only some $940,600 worth of works. In May 1895 the Governor, acting under the authority of an earlier Railway Act of 1881, took possession of the line and plant and took over the running and control of the constructed portion of line, as well as the Belgrove-Motupiki and Springfield-Otarama sections totalling 14 miles, for which contracts had been let by the Company.

There was a long series of law suits brought by debentureholders against the Crown, but they lost all the way through to the Privy Council in England. So it was that the Midland Railway Company eventually, ignominiously and expensively, slowly and painfully, came to an end. The Company had been too optimistic in hoping to be able to complete a line of railway so fraught with physical difficulties; eventually even the Government itself abandoned some portions as being too difficult and uneconomic, and the takeover of the Company, seen in retrospect, marked the practical end of the Nelson Railway insofar as its connection to the Midland Railway was concerned. The two cannot be considered together after this event.

After the Government took over the line, progress was still slow for a number of years, doubtless at first because of the uncertainty of the legal position governing the Company *vis-à-vis* the Government. In the 1895 Public Works Statement it was recorded that the Jacksons-Otira section was nearing completion, and in December 1899 trains began running up to Otira. The western side of the line was complete.

Work from Springfield commenced in 1898, though the question of the mountain route was still largely unsolved, and in 1899 rails were laid from Springfield on about a mile of the old Company formation. In reporting on the Otira-Bealey section, the Government decided that the Company's proposals for a 1 in 15 ascent of Arthur's Pass by Fell engine was definitely not to be recommended, and no one could argue with that. It would have been a catastrophe had the Midland Line been forced to handle all its traffic with such a line. Over the next few years work proceeded slowly on the difficult formation work from Springfield, through Staircase and Pattersons Creek Gullies and on towards Broken River.

Canterbury was becoming impatient at the slow progress. In 1904 agitation, which had been dormant, flared up again assisted by a few well placed hints by Premier Seddon that if the railway was to be completed, more vocal effort would be necessary. This must be one of the few recorded instances of a Prime Minister inviting criticism of Government works! Combined Canterbury-Westland conferences followed, and strong resolutions were passed calling on the Government to complete the project. A massive deputation went to Wellington and waited on the Government, and sympathetic consideration was promised by Mr Seddon. By 1907 the Springfield-Broken River section had been completed and West Coast passengers could travel to Christchurch by rail, coach and rail again, in one day.

The first shot for the Otira Tunnel was officially fired by Prime Minister Sir Joseph Ward on 5 May 1908, at Otira. The mighty undertaking was under way, with a contract for $1,199,588 let to J. McLean & Sons, a firm who had had considerable engineering experience throughout the country, including the Auckland Tramways, Rotorua railway portions, and parts of the Northern Railway beyond Helensville, in addition to bridge and harbour construction works.

Whatever Canterbury and Westland may have felt about the project, in some parts of the country enthusiasm was not so warm. The *Dominion* in its report of the ceremony marking the firing of the first shot reported:

A WHITE ELEPHANT

It was not unfit that the elements should have conspired to invest with the most dismal circumstances the official firing of the first shot. The weeping skies ... were of ominous significance. The occasion produced the expected volume of statistics and tall talk from the Premier, and the inevitable references to "an epoch" and "a great national work" from everybody who spoke, but we regard it as an occasion giving little cause for rejoicing.

After an initially promising start, considerable difficulties were encountered by the contractors in the way of crumbling shale and rotten rock which required massive and costly timbering work, and in two years only one mile of heading was excavated. By 1912, the contract should have been completed, but another three miles and 42 chains lay between the two completely excavated headings and the contractors asked the Government to relieve them of the job.

The Government took over, but the intervention of the First World War considerably delayed work which, up to then, had seen the completion of the line to Arthur's Pass with the exception of the Bealey Bridge. Throughout the war years work, slowed by a lack of manpower, interior flooding, and loose shale, proceeded slowly on through the heart of the mountains. On 21 August 1918, the headings met and a ceremony was held at the faces, only 1⅛ inch out in level and ¾ inch in alignment. By October 1921, the tunnel lining was complete and in May 1923 the great project was finally completed and the West and East Coasts of the South Island, at a cost of $4,360,768, were linked by railway. The dreams of 63 years before had become a reality.

Today the Midland Line (in common use the name is now generally applied only to the Rolleston-Arthur's Pass section of 73 miles) is one of the most vital links in the whole transportation pattern of the country. The importance of the line was demonstrated vividly in 1951 when on 18 April part of the Kowhai Viaduct was washed away in a tremendous flood. While gangs laboured day and night to repair the break, fleets of motor trucks had to be mobilised via the Lewis Pass to Reefton, taking mails, perishables, and foodstuffs to the Coast, and backloading coal. After the road, which had also been damaged by flood, was repaired, convoys inched their way between the Springfield and Kowhai Bush railheads. The comparison between the two methods is impressive: the trucks took two weeks to do what the railway normally did in two days of operation. It is events such as this that dramatise the indispensable place that the railways have in the national transport system, and that the Midland Line in particular has in the South Island.

It is by train that the vast resources of the West Coast roll through the Tunnel every day in long strings of coal, timber, and produce, while trainloads of empties and manufactured goods move east-west to the Coast. It was on a train of the latter type that I had a footplate trip over the most picturesque section of the line, from Springfield up to the Pass on the largest steam locomotive class ever built for the New Zealand Railways, the power-packed Kb.

It was No 965, the first number in the class, that awaited me at Springfield on a dreary grey day in January 1966. The drizzle drifted in from the hills as the crew checked the big engine while steam swirled from seemingly its every part. In the firebox the flames were flickering and dancing among the piles of red hot coals on the 47·7-square foot fire grate, the largest (at the time the Kb was built) of any handfired engine in the world. Unlike the K and Ka classes of the North Island, the Kb has always been a coalburner, and until a fireman knows how to fire a Kb properly he becomes a very tired man indeed. The Kb's capacity for coal when working up the grades on the Midland Line, seems virtually inexhaustible.

With dieselisation coming increasingly closer, maintenance on 965 seemed to have been kept to a minimum, and she was rather a sorry sight. Soot and grease covered the boiler and lagging was coming off many of the steam pipes. The numberplate was so badly tarnished that from more than 10 feet it was impossible to read the number, let alone the class letters. It is a tribute to their designer that the Kbs still run as well as they do. They may be pretty scruffy externally, but they still have plenty of heart for the steep grades of the Midland Line. At 600 tons load rating they have a 20-ton edge on the latest Di diesel, while the Dg class diesels, to quote one of the Springfield station staff "are just useless up here". Train 183, which the Kb was to take up to the Pass was late in arriving, but made up for it by her entrance to the station. The faint blast of a distant whistle soon gave way to a plume of white smoke that grew rapidly larger until Kb969 topped the grade down by the engine shed and charged into the yards in a flurry of steam and smoke, the squealing brakeblocks sparking off the rumbling wheels and the couplings banged and crashed while the train shuddered to a halt.

Our engine's brakes sighed off as we rolled down the loop to replace 969 backing off to the engine shed for her fires to be cleaned. A few minutes later the whistle howled, the pistons strained, and the exhaust belched smoke towards the clearing sky as the Kb got her 300-ton train moving out of Springfield and headed for the hills.

At first the line is relatively easy going but soon past Kowhai Bush the first foothills of the Torlesse Range are encountered. The Kb was punching forth smoke like Vesuvius in eruption as we bit into the first real grades, and the solid sound of the exhaust settled down to a rhythmic thud as we ran past the first magnificent views of the Waimakariri Gorge, where far below the river meandered its way to the plains and dwarflike beeches grew like scenery on a model railway. Great rocky hillsides rose from the blue-green waters of the river and soon the Kb was right in amongst them, surging along with a full head of steam while little pieces of coal trickled down from the tender and unerringly lodged down the back of my neck.

The Kb is a very dirty engine to work on; coaldust and flecks fly everywhere, while the tremendous volume of smoke with its soot particles is simply hell in the tunnels on the line. Up until the time I had my first Kb ride tunnels had never bothered me much and it was almost with superior amusement that I watched the fireman pull his jacket over his face as we approached the first one. Less than five seconds later as I coughed and spluttered I had to admit shamefacedly to myself that perhaps I wasn't as experienced as I'd thought.

The smoke put out by a Kb is simply tremendous when the engine is working, particularly so when the smoke is trapped by the narrow "tube" of a tunnel. I hastily stuffed a handkerchief into my mouth — I could hardly breathe, but that was better than a second longer of Kb soot down my throat. For the remainder of the 16 tunnels on the line I kept the increasingly grimy handkerchief firmly rammed down my gullet, and each tunnel seemed to develop into a contest between the Kb and myself as to whether I could hold my breath for the length of time it seemed to take to pound through each. Crews on the line received at the time I made my trip, 24c per day tunnel allowance, and it was money I didn't envy them. They certainly earned it. I looked like a refugee from a minstrel show by the time we rocketed out of the last tunnel.

The Kb, despite her light load, was making heavy weather up towards Avoca and the needle was steady at 10 mph. At Avoca we left the gorge behind and slogged up through the hills towards Cragieburn, the brown tussock-covered valley floor lit, as the clouds cleared, with the orange rays of the dying sun. Ahead of us reared the massive peaks of the Southern Alps, flecks of snow and ice relieving the blue shadows of their scarred sides.

The Kb plugged wearily round the curve into Cass, 1,862 feet above sea level, and drew slowly up beside the water tank, from which over 2,000 gallons of water splashed into her tender. We shunted off a couple of wagons, and with the clang of the shovel against the mouth of the firebox, throttled off out of Cass until we joined up with the river again, this time to run along the bank instead of dizzy feet up a cliff face as we had previously.

In a rattle of wheels we swung out over the bridge where on the far bank the old ballast siding ran off up the river and the crumbling remains of an old guard's van kept a silent vigil beside the trickling waters. Past Cora Lynn, and the engine beat out its rhythm of power as we steamed on beside mountain beeches whose branches whipped past the cab windows. As the twilight settled over the peaceful valley the only sound was the muffled bellow from the stack and the rumble of the train's passing as we finally made our way up the last grade and drew into Arthur's Pass, the lights of cabins and chalets beginning to wink out through the trees. It was time to unhook Kb965, turn her, and clean the fire ready for the next train back to Springfield.

The Kbs are mighty engines, and they work in country as ruggedly magnificent as they themselves are. The Midland Line is a tough hard track, but with some of the best scenery on the New Zealand Railways. The old Kbs, as they slog their way up to the Pass, are an integral part of this scenic magnificence. When they go, when the blast of a whistle echoing through the gorge is heard no more, when the viaducts no longer reverberate with the weight of 146 tons of Kb, then will be closed the most interesting and magnificent chapter in the story of the Midland Line.

13

No noise, no effort

FOR ALL ITS OBVIOUS and superior operating ability, electric traction in New Zealand has been very much a circumstantial affair, used only when force of circumstances rendered other forms of motive power impracticable. There are only 68 miles of electrified track in the whole country: the Wellington suburban area, the Lyttelton line, and the Arthur's Pass-Otira section. Despite the small mileage and the comparatively few locomotive classes and their lack of numerical strength, the electric locomotives of the New Zealand Railways have given outstanding service. Their praises largely unsung, the electric locomotives and "units" daily move 7½ per cent of New Zealand's railway traffic on only 2½ per cent of the total track mileage.

The Otira Tunnel was responsible for the introduction of electric traction into New Zealand. The section from Otira (1,248 feet) to Arthur's Pass (2,433 feet) is on an average grade of 1 in 37¼ with a ruling gradient in the tunnel of 1 in 33 up to the Pass. Because of the 5 miles 26 chains length of the Tunnel, steam locomotives on such a grade were obviously impracticable.

That electric traction was practicable had been demonstrated as early as 1890 on the City and South London Railway, the first deep-level tube line in the world. Further success, this time with the electrification of an ordinary tunnel, was shown by the Baltimore and Ohio Railroad in the United States. Indeed railway electrification had first been demonstrated as early as 1879 by German engineer von Siemens, who produced a passenger locomotive for use at the Berlin Trades Fair of that year. The tram and trolley lines of the world had also demonstrated the striking practicability of the application of electricity to railed vehicles.

Early in 1916 instructions were given for the preparation of an electrification scheme for the Otira area. Three schemes were drawn up: (a) the tunnel and approaches, (b) Jacksons to Cass, and (c) Jacksons to Springfield. The type of electrification was also to be considered. Basically three types are possible: alternating current, one-phase; alternating current, three-phase; or, direct current. In Europe in particular, the AC one-phase has become popular, with very high voltages, up to 25,000 on some systems.

The three-phase AC involves double overhead conductors and the return of current through the running rails, and involves great complication at junctions. It is expensive to install, and the only system over which it has been used to any extent is the Italian Railways which later reconverted much of their line to DC because of the difficulties they had encountered.

The majority of established systems in the world use direct current, generally from overhead conductors, at voltages of 1,500 to 3,000, though the extensive electrification of the Southern Region of British Railways is third-rail at 600 volts. The disadvantage of DC systems is that the distance over which current can be conducted is lower than with AC systems, where sub-stations are less frequent.

The 1916 report recommended 1,500 volts DC as the standard to be adopted for New Zealand, that being considered the most suitable voltage and the DC conduction being considered superior for haulage purposes. With the splendid service that the Eo class electric locomotives have given, the choice has been vindicated many times over.

The route to be electrified, because of capital cost and the fact that electrification was a new experience for New Zealand, was kept to the minimum and only the Arthur's Pass-Otira section was electrified. A further consideration that affected the decision was that larger electrification depended upon the completion of the Lake Coleridge hydro scheme and the coal power-station initially used could not have generated sufficient current for a larger project. The total length of the Otira scheme is 8 miles 32 chains, which was considered adequate for the two 1,200 kW turbo sets of the old Otira steam plant in operation until 1941.

New Zealand's first electric locomotives were the five English Electric Eo class, ordered in 1921 and after nearly half a century of service they are only now being considered for replacement, tenders having been called in August 1966.

It is perhaps surprising that they should have been replaced because, with the changeover to diesels in a few years, the need for electrification of the Tunnel would appear to be redundant and there is no readily discernible reason why diesels should not be able to operate straight through from Christchurch to Greymouth in due course. However, the isolated electrified line is to be continued. If there were plans for the extension of electrification it might well be a different story – and no doubt a more successful one.

The Eo locomotives were built at the Preston works of the English Electric Company and their capacity was based upon an estimated 1,000 tons per day eastbound and 700 westbound. It was envisaged that five locomotives would cope with such tonnages but that eventually a total of eight would be required. Today the Eos handle daily tonnages of 4,500 with peak periods of over 5,000 tons, and the same five engines still tackle all the trains that roll through the Otira Tunnel. The engines are equipped with the standard English Electric DK82 motor, totally enclosed; they use forced ventilation and develop a starting tractive effort per unit of 25,000 lb with a one-hour rating of 14,200 hp. The motors, wound for 750v, are connected in permanent series. Current collection from the overhead is by air-operated pantographs, raised by compressed air and floated on springs. The articulated four-wheel bogies, two per unit, ensure that none of the tractive force is taken through the underframe.

With a working life approaching that of the Ab, the Eo is a locomotive as remarkable in its own way as ever the Ab was, and it was with considerable interest that I swung aboard the three-locomotive unit that at the head of an express was my first introduction to electric engines. The Eo has a cramped little cab, right of centre of the locomotive, with the driver's seat and a small jump seat, but on this trip I had the more spacious accommodation of a jump seat in front of the entrance door, in the main body of the locomotive, the driver's cab being enclosed. Behind me stretched the banks and relays, giving forth loud bangs and mysterious thumps from time to time. Ominous notices of warning of the dangers of electricity and the methods and merits of resuscitation, were placed conspicuously on the bulkhead behind me. I hoped facetiously that I would have no need to study them, and that a bunch of delinquent volts would not decide to jump me in the darkness of the tunnel.

Once we were under way it was relatively quiet, and although the ride was surprisingly rough I could enjoy the unsurpassed view that the front of an electric on the climb to the Tunnel can provide. Ahead ran the track, rising towards the snowcapped rugged mountain fastness that reared up ahead of us. To the left the boulder-strewn river-bed indicated the torrents that could suddenly sweep down, though only a trickle of ice-cold water was splashing over the warm rocks at that time. The bushclad slopes fell away on either side as we advanced up the valley toward the crags and peaks of the Alps. It was hard not to imagine that this was some alpine railway in Switzerland. The run up to the Otira Tunnel mouth would be considerable compensation to the driver for the boring run through the Tunnel. We rounded a bend, the mouth of the Tunnel came into view around the corner of the substation, and then we rattled into the damp blackness of the Tunnel.

The ride through it is interesting on the first occasion, as water drips from stalactites hanging from the roof, and the headlight beams ahead up the steep track. After that it becomes rather monotonous; while after three trips in the Eo I began to wonder how the drivers stuck out their six-week shift before going on to a two-week spell of duty on the Otira steam roster. Two drivers operate the locomotives, permanently used in a multiple unit of three locomotives, the others being held in reserve or away for servicing. The use of two drivers, one at each end, is a purely checking procedure in the event of any mishap in the Tunnel.

I did two trips on Eo4 and one on Eo6, the latter on a goods train from the Pass down to Otira and on this last occasion, at the invitation of the driver, I wedged myself into the little cab for a look at the controls. The control gear is of the simple English Electric camshaft variety, an all-electric system avoiding air valves and interlocks. A series of cams is mounted on a shaft, rotated by a small motor by means of worm gearing. These operate the contactors for cutting out the starting resistance and effecting the series and parallel of the motors which control the power and speed of the locomotive.

These locomotives have Westinghouse straight and automatic air brakes, hand brakes, and rheostatic brakes. The latter create resistances controlled by the appropriate controller handle in the cab and limit the downward speed of trains to 26 mph. Standby batteries are also carried to provide energy for control gear and compressor motor at 120v. This battery supply is sufficient to enable the engine to make a complete trip and allows the driver to use both air and rheostatic brakes in the event of a failure of the overhead supply.

The Eo is a simple engine from the driver's viewpoint, indeed in descending the Tunnel the controller is simply left in the second notch and the rheostatic brake applied, the driver thereafter being merely a safety device in what is virtually an automatically controlled descent. The speed limit of 26 mph does nothing to enliven the trip, and the 8·3 miles are normally allowed 30 minutes on the timetable. Slow, methodical progression though it may be, the Eo locomotives are some of the best workhorses on the railways, and they are surely an eloquent tribute to their designers. With no noise and no apparent effort, they typify the best in electric traction: hardworking, durable, powerful and longlived.

It was the undoubted success of the Eo class that led to the decision to electrify the 1·6 miles long Lyttelton Tunnel, which for 61 years had been steam worked until electrification was completed and the system went over to the Ec class engines on 14 February 1929. Again it was largely circumstances, the long tunnel, that prompted the decision. The electrified mileage of 10·8 miles included some 4·3 miles of double track on the 6·4 mile-long line to the Port. The tried and proven English Electric Company (after tenders had been received from England, Europe, and America) was again awarded the contract, and the six 50-ton Bo-Bo type locomotives are still going strong though approaching the mature 40 year age-mark.

With an initial tractive effort some 3,000 lb higher than the Eo but with a rated hourly tractive effort of some 2,600 lb less, the Ec class engines are well equipped to handle suburban and freight trains on a line having far less severe grades than the Otira section. The engines have a driving compartment at each end, with a master control, brake and auxiliary controls and pantograph raising cocks. The driver sits in the middle of the cab but rear view mirrors on each side give a clear view of shunting or guard's signals. The master control is rather similar to that found on tramcars, except that it is on a smaller scale and the handle itself is fitted with a "deadman's" device whereby the removal of the driver's hand automatically cuts off the power and applies the main brakes. The Ec class appear to be good for several more years of work yet.

Hitherto in New Zealand's electric traction development, passenger trains had been locomotive-hauled and consisted of normal passenger stock, but the advent of the Wellington-Johnsonville electrification in 1938 saw the appearance of multiple-unit stock in distinctive blue livery with bright silver bands, and a new era in suburban passenger transport was opened. Again it was English Electric who supplied the six motor coaches and six trailers, and soon the units of motor and trailer were a familiar sight as they whined up the steep grades and curves of the line to Johnsonville, clipping some eight minutes off the previous steam schedule though the stops had been increased from two to four. The most impressive statistic was the increase from 700,000 to over two million

Top: The long climb has finished and the relieved fireman puts his head out into the cooling drizzle as the last of the We class, 375, rounds the curve into Rewanui after the gruelling slog up from Dunollie.

Centre: We375 sends white steam blasting up to join the mountain mist as she makes ready to shunt her train ready to jog down the grade from Rewanui. These powerful tank engines manage 100 tons up the 1 in 26 grade.

Bottom: One of several A class engines still giving sterling service on the West Coast is 472, awaiting repairs in January 1966. Behind her nuzzles a Wf seeking company on what may well prove to be the scrap track.

Top left: Fussing importantly at the head of the early morning Mixed Train to Rewanui is Ww679, on which the author made the exhilarating climb up the centre-rail incline. The raised section in the cowcatcher was for clearing the Fell rail.

Top right: Half-hidden in mist and rain on a summer day at Kumara on the Ross line, sits Ab610 at the head of the afternoon Mixed Train to Greymouth; she is waiting to cross her opposite number bound for Ross.

Bottom: Ab755 with a Greymouth-bound goods train staggers up the last of the serpentine grade into Kumara.

passengers carried per annum within a short time of the "units" being put into service. In less impressive livery of Midland red and Wellington grease-brown, the units still labour up the Johnsonville line, giving an essential service to the ever-growing suburban communities in the area.

At the time of the Otira electrification, one of the sections of track that it was estimated would benefit from electrification was the Paekakariki-Wellington section, and in 1940 this 24½-mile stretch of line went electric. The steep gradients on the Plimmerton section and the 2½-mile-long Tawa deviation tunnel were the deciding factors.

To work the line, locomotives of the unusual 1-D-2 wheel arrangement were built. The first, classified Ed101, was built by English Electric, and a further seven were built in 1939 and 1940 at Hutt, using electrical equipment supplied by English Electric. At 87·4 tons these engines were fractionally lighter than the English built one. Later two more were built at Addington and entered service in 1941.

A curious feature of Ed101 was the "skirt" (later removed) concealing the wheels, a typical feature of steam tramway engine construction when such skirts were designed to hide the valve motion to preserve the disguise of electrification. The use of a skirt on this main line electric engine was curious to say the least. Ed101 also had three gold stripes which have since been painted over.

These powerful but rather cumbersome engines are rated for 500-ton goods and 400-ton passenger trains, though their heavy axle loading did nothing when at speed to help preserve track, and they are now confined almost exclusively to freight services. The units ordered for the Paekakariki line were similar to those on the Johnsonville section, but are normally made up of a driving trailer, motor coach and driving trailer, coupled in multiples of 6- or 9-total if necessary. Their introduction knocked 10 minutes off the previous steam schedule of 59 minutes and allowed for three more intermediate stops.

The most handsome electric locomotives in New Zealand, and one of the most capable locomotives working in New Zealand today are indisputably the superb Ew class engines. They have an articulated design, of three four-wheel bogies, the articulation being over the centre bogie, similar to the design of the later Drewry railcars. The Ew packs 1,800 hp into its 75-ton weight, almost 500 tractive hp more than the Da of nearly the same tonnage. Again products of English Electric, they are rated up to 1,000 tons of goods and 500-ton passenger trains, and with their tractive effort of 42,300 lb at starting, they have almost 25 per cent as much again as the tractive effort of a Ka. More than one driver has pronounced them as being "the most comfortable engine to work on the New Zealand Railways". Their ability to work long periods without replacement of wheel tyres and their general overall simplicity of maintenance make them ideal locomotives from an operating viewpoint. Today, they work trains on both the Paekakariki and Hutt Valley lines with consummate ease.

"I am convinced that complete electrification between Auckland and Wellington will be entirely self-supporting, and the investigations carried out so far have forced me to the conclusion that, without it, we will have the greatest difficulty in getting goods through the Main Trunk in 10 years' time unless we carry out expensive duplication works of both tracks and tunnels." With these words the then General Manager of the Railways Department (F. W. Aicken) stated in 1949 what was intended to be the future trend in electric traction in New Zealand. Shortly afterwards he left for an intensive study tour overseas to consider all aspects of electrification. At that time it was intended that Auckland would get an electric suburban service as soon as it could be arranged. The Auckland-Frankton electrification had been described as "a definite commitment". It was even intended that contracts for the Auckland work might be negotiated by Mr Aicken while he was overseas.

This grand scheme however, came to nought. In many ways a pity, because while without disparaging in any way the work that diesel electrics are doing on the Main Trunk, straight electrics could doubtless have done the task even better. There is no doubt that it would have been a costly project, and perhaps might not have paid for itself for many years, but a motive power trend that seems likely to outlast the longevity record of steam, would have been available for the far foreseeable future. The change of management not long afterwards, followed by the retirement and replacement of the Chief Mechanical Engineer by a man with less apprehension about the state of the railways' motive power, resulted in the top priority status being stripped from electrification until, with the increasing use of diesels, the pressing necessity began to be resolved by the new beef added to the locomotive fleet. For some time however the diesels were regarded as merely a stopgap until electrification could be proceeded with, though this view appears to have been cast aside long since.

The opening of the final stage of the Hutt Valley electrification scheme to Upper Hutt on 24 July 1955 marked the completion of electric services in New Zealand with the exception of the Mana realignment of the Paekakariki line. With Main Trunk proposals shelved for the immediate future at least, it is difficult to envisage any further large-scale electrification work being put in hand. There is agitation for electric services to be extended at least as far as Paraparaumu and possibly Otaki, but other than this the pattern appears reasonably complete.

Electric lines in New Zealand are only a small portion of the total, but over them flows a tremendous tonnage of both passengers and freight. Insignificant in terms of mileage though they may be, and numerically few the locomotives that run over them, the electrified lines of the New Zealand Railways and their rolling-stock play a part in the economy and transport pattern of the country that is of a vital significance, and one which will undoubtedly increase still further in proportion, as the years pass.

14

Steam in the deep south

EVEN THE MOST CASUAL GLANCE at a map of the Southland Province cannot fail to register the complex network of railways that reach into the heart of these fertile farmlands, and so tantalisingly brush the fringes of the high country. The Southland area with its many little branch lines – several closed only recently – and its still total reliance on steam power outside the limits of the Invercargill yards, makes a trip to the province a must for any who delight in trailing white smoke plumes and the solid punch of smoke emptying from a stack as a train grinds slowly up a grade. High speed running is not just the prerogative of Canterbury engines either, and a run on a train making up time to Invercargill can provide a feast of excitement as the driver races the clock across the Mataura Plains.

It was in such a helter-skelter hell-for-leather fashion that I first entered Southland. I was travelling as a passenger on the South Island Limited when I received notice of the potential for high-speed travel that Southland can provide. We were 14 minutes late when the whistle shrilled and the Ja drew her 13-total train out of Clinton, and by Waipahi 10 miles further on we had somehow lost another one and a half minutes. It was as if the crew and the engine suddenly realised that they were going to be late into the City. The regulator was opened rapidly and in no time the quarter-mile pegs were whipping past at four to the minute, 60 mph, as the train howled its way towards Gore. From Waipahi the time-table allows 28 minutes to reach Gore 22 miles away. Just an even 22 minutes after the whistle had sounded at Waipahi we were sliding to a stop at Gore – we had made up six minutes, and the engine could be heard panting feverishly as she awaited the departure signal. But it was to no avail, van work cost five minutes longer than allowed in the table, and we were a massive 16½ minutes late when the engine took up the strain at 7.25 plus 30 seconds.

The Ja soon had the train up to 45; then 50, and in a few miles the posts were again tearing past at 60 as mile after mile whipped by beneath the racing wheels. Further delays unfortunately resulted at Mataura and the train was still 16 minutes late when the piercing blast of the departure whistle echoed around the yards. As we cleared the yards the exhaust was settling down to its staccato rhythm and in a matter of three miles the Ja was again clicking along at just over the 60 mark. A slight grade saw speed fall to 45, but soon it was picking up again until it was time for the brakes to slide against the whirring wheels to stop at Edendale. The station agent seemed to sense the race, and the station bell clanged urgently to be followed, while the echo still hung in the air, by the impatient blast of the locomotive's whistle as the steam poured into the cylinders and the driving wheels began to turn. We were now only 10½ minutes late, having made up five and a half minutes in only nine miles – the race was well and truly on.

The grade south of Edendale slowed the panting engine, but speed never fell below 30 mph as the drifting black smoke poured back over the train. Soon speed was picking up again, and several little whistle stops passed by in a blur of buildings as the speed crept up. Despite her efforts, the Ja had lost a minute on the grade, and at 8.8 p.m. we were now 11 minutes late as we whistled out of Woodlands.

Eleven miles to go, and only 12 minutes before the arrival time of 8.20 p.m. at Invercargill would show on the clock. Time seemed to be winning. But the crew and their engine were obviously not to be discouraged and were away with a will as the Ja dragged her load of some 400 tons up to and past the 50 reading. The countryside slid past in a blur, the thunder of noise up ahead bespoke the efforts being made and my eyes strained for the tell-tale white pegs flashing past. Soon houses were zipping by as the frenzied pace was sustained, but the hands of the clock were on 8.19.

At 8.20 we were well inside the City boundary and the first gentle brake pressure could be felt. Then suddenly the brakes gripped harder and the carriage shuddered as the speed fell rapidly away. It was obviously a signal check, and the whistle blast that the Ja flung at the offending signal must have been heard from one end of Invercargill to the other.

It worked though. The brake pressure eased and the engine opened up again as crossing bells clanged past the window. Another precious minute had been lost, and a three-minute-late entry became four as we stopped by the platform. Officially we were four minutes late, but what a mighty effort had gone into the reduction to that time! It was a splendid example of the ability of a well-maintained steam engine to make up time, and it was an impressive introduction to Southern steam.

At the time of writing the only diesels in Southland are the Ds yard-shunting engines, still regarded with a jaundiced eye by shunters who liked the crisp work of a Wf on the yard shunt. The antiquated old roundhouse dating from 1882 is now a thing of the past, and Southern steamers bed down in the most modern steam shed in the country, with five tracks accommodating up to 10 Jas at one time. The faithful A and Ab classes still give good service and the Wf has not yet fully retired from the shunt. Until recent years even nineteenth century vintage F class tanks were to be seen at work in the yards. Invercargill is still a stronghold of steam, and wonderfully well it continues to be served by its engines.

The history of steam in Southland has not always been so praiseworthy. Railways in the province date back to 1863 when ordinances were passed reserving areas of land for the Bluff-Invercargill and Oreti railways. In the following year a small section of the Bluff line was completed, but financial difficulties soon loomed large and not until February 1867, three years and two contracts later, was the line opened for service.

Southland's great fiasco however was the infamous wooden-railed Makarewa proposition. An Australian engineer, J. R. Davies, claimed that he could build a wooden-railed line to Makarewa, eight miles, in less time and at less cost than a line of iron rails. The rail was 8-by-8-inch square timber, the flangeless rolling-stock having inclined guide wheels to direct it. The idea appealed to the now financially conscious Provincial Council and the scheme went ahead. Rails which had proved adequate in Australia's dry climate were to prove no match however for the rains of Southland. The first trip over the line was recorded as being "a bit rough" but as goods traffic was the prime consideration, such complaints went unheeded.

Following considerable public agitation, it was decided to hold a People's Day, and allow the Great Unwashed a free trip over the new engineering marvel. The 25 October 1864 dawned warm and sunny, and several trains of excited Southlanders were despatched to Makarewa. Rain soon threatened, and while two trains were got back to Invercargill, the remainder were less fortunate.

The rain made the rails so spongy, that the engine wheels could not grip, and sanding proved of no avail. The final insult was the harnessing of cart-horses to the trains and so the sorry processions wound their damp way back to town.

It is recorded that at one of many stops required to give the horses a spell an old lady got out of the train and began to walk. Officials hastened over to ask her to board the train as it was to leave shortly.

"Dinna ye fuss," was her reply, "I'm in a hurry! I'll walk on ahead and tell them ye be coming."

The rails soon proved totally inadequate, and the whole sorry fiasco, which had descended to permanent horsepower, was pulled up and replaced with iron rails in 1867. It had been an expensive lesson.

Southland's first railways had been built to the world standard gauge of 4 feet 8½ inches but the Public Works Act of 1870 which had decreed 3 feet 6 inches as the New Zealand gauge resulted in conversion of the Bluff and Makarewa lines, the latter having meantime been extended to Winton. Progress was rapid under Central Government control and the pattern of the South's railways developed steadily.

By 1878 Kingston had been reached, 1879 saw the Invercargill-Christchurch link-up, while the private company known as the Waimea Plains Railway Company completed the Lumsden-Gore link in 1880, eventually to be purchased by the Government six years later. The eighties and nineties saw rails reach Wairio, Browns, Glenham, Mossburn and, after the turn of the century, Waikaia, Tokonui, Waikaka, Tuatapere, and finally, in 1925, Orawia. The complex pattern was complete. Inevitably the reverse trend set in and 1959-66 saw several of the little lines farewell their last train.

The most impressive farewell was undoubtedly that accorded to the last train on the Seaward Bush line, the branch to Tokonui closed in January 1966. The great day of farewell dawned as anxious railway officials received news that some locals had vowed the last train would never leave Tokonui. It was feared that some rails might be lifted, so the police were called in to keep watch. An inspection revealed that all was well, and amid hearty farewells the train whistled out of the station, with several cars of passengers and some wagons in tow.

There was a steep grade out of Tokonui and the engine headed into it with white plumes flying. Suddenly the wheels skidded madly and the exhaust noise went haywire as the driver frantically grabbed for the brake lever. For a distance of some yards the rails were inches thick in axle-grease! The crew made haste to scrape it off, but it had been applied with an expert hand. It was impossible to remove it completely, and the engine wheels spun viciously and uselessly. The worried guard and engine crew conferred and eventually decided to run back and ring Train Control from Tokonui.

As the train backed into the station it had so recently left the guard alighted and picked up the Train Control phone. It was dead. The linesmen, knowing the train was to be the last, had already removed the wires. There was no help for it. Over to the post office went the guard and through went a toll call to Control. The situation was explained. Then, as on the field of Balaclava, came the command: "Charge!"

So charge it was to be. The wagons were left at the station, fat passengers trembled in case they too should suffer the same fate, and the fireman built up his fire in readiness. Once more the departure whistle shrilled. The engine opened out, and exhaust roaring, couplings crashing, drivers churning, she hurtled up the grade, staggered and slipped, bucked and fought her triumphant way over the greasy rails until with an exultant whistle blast, she headed thankfully off towards Invercargill.

Not all the Southland branches have suffered closure. The Wairio branch which connects with the Ohai Railway Board's private line sees many long coal trains depart for Invercargill and the Bluff, while most of the other remaining lines still see two or three trains a week with seasonal extras when the traffic warrants.

The real rags-to-riches story though is that of the little Mossburn branch line, 12 miles long, that leaves the Kingston branch just north of Lumsden. Built in 1886-7, closed to passengers in 1937 and serving only two flag stations and a terminal structure at Mossburn, the branch had long languished half-forgotten, seeing only two or three trains a week when an old A would trundle through the paddocks with a van, a few stock wagons, and perhaps some lime or timber.

Then came the Manapouri Scheme with its demand for thousands of tons of material. Today Mossburn as the railhead for the Scheme often sees in a day more trains than it previously catered for in a week as Abs wheel in trainloads of steel and supplies for the tough road haul through to the construction works. No longer a flag terminus, Mossburn has a new station, a new goods shed, its own Tr shunting tractor and the first stationmaster in its history – who, incidentally, besides having this distinction, was the last stationmaster on the now defunct Waimate branch. Business is booming and the Department's officers in Southland are confident that business will continue, even after the Scheme is completed, as more of the back country is opened up.

It was on another branch that I sampled Southern steam from the footplate, this time on an Ab working the return goods run up to Kingston, Trains 667 and 668. Though it was summer at the time, cold misty rain drifted over the yards, spattered on the wagons and caused the shivering shunters to pull their coats more firmly around them as the cool breeze swept around their legs. At the head of the train of eight La open wagons, two of them full of coal for the New Zealand Railways Lake Wakatipu steamship *Earnslaw*, Ab784 stood half obscured in drifting steam as the clang of the shovel could be heard above the thumping of the Westinghouse pump. In the freezing guard's van in which I was travelling for the first part of the trip, the guard miserably surveyed the cleaner's note, "Sorry no fire, but lost my matches", and cursed the Railways, the rain, and the unfortunate cleaner.

At 6.45 a.m. the green flag waved and with a jerk the Ab set off out of the yards. Steam swirled all round her in a machine-made mist of white against the grey background of Nature's darker patterns, and soon we were clattering along over the small section of CTC-controlled track, the green signals gleaming through the rain as we headed northwards.

Gradually the mist began to lift, and when we bumped to a halt at Makarewa to unload some parcels from the van the threatening skies had lifted considerably. The Ab fussed around shunting off two wagons and then came a steady run up to Winton where the load was again reduced by two wagons. After a stop at Centre Bush for more van traffic we chuffed slowly into Dipton where, at the kind invitation of the crew, I joined them on the engine. What a blessed relief it was to stand in the warm glow radiating from the firebox as the old engine heaved and panted vigorously and another cold squall swept over the train.

At 9.20 the regulator was opened and 784 moved off towards Lumsden. The track was rough and the engine poorly sprung, jolting her way along in a succession of bonejarring thumps from rail joint to rail joint as if determined to hammer herself and the track down into the ballast. At Lumsden the local crew took over the train and two splendid fellows they were too, who made me very much at home on their engine. As it was 10 a.m. morning tea was in order, but first of course dirty hands must be washed.

It is doubtful if there is a more versatile tool than the railway fireman's shovel. When washed off with the hot water hose it makes a wonderful skillet for cooking steak, making toast or, as on this occasion, it will serve as a washbasin. The deep sides, water from the boiler and some soap give a hot wash as good as any to be obtained in the most modern family bathroom! Incidentally, it can also be used for shovelling coal on to a fire. It is not only the shovel that can be used for cooking, though; a parcel of sausages wrapped in greaseproof paper, a pie, soup, or what-you-will placed up on top of the firebox at the start of a shift will produce a superb meal by the time dinner or supper rolls round. The life of a steam locomotive crew isn't all soot and hard work.

Some 20 minutes later the driver tugged the whistle-cord and opened the regulator, the wheels spun for a few turns and then settled down as we clanked slowly off up the grade from Lumsden with our diminutive train bucking along in the rear. Old 784 may have had only a light load but she was "forty years on" and still took the grades pretty vigorously. After a mile and some chains we clanked slowly to a halt at Mararoa Junction, simply the name given to the point on the tracks at which the Mossburn branch heads off over the old wooden combined bridge built across the Oreti River. The guard, accompanied by a small boy who was going fishing up at Kingston, climbed down from the van and trudged up the slope to unlock the points which had been left set for Mossburn.

A slight drizzle was still falling and the rails were greasy as the old Ab skittered like a mare when the driver opened the throttle, but soon we were climbing steadily away up the grade again on the weed-grown line to Kingston. The engine handled the grade well though my fireman friend was occupied for several minutes as his shovel rang on the firebox mouth and each scoop shot into the flames.

As the sweet thick smell of coal-smoke and oil filled the cab and my mouth, we galloped along beside the Oreti, past glades of green willow trees overhanging the track which constantly whipped against the smokebox until the black boiler and stack of old 784 were resplendent in bright green fronds that had pulled from the trees. The rain had eased as we rocked through Lowther, 55 miles out from Invercargill. The countryside was losing its fresh green look and giving way to the brown grass of the hills. Old 784 was suffering from a clogged fire and not steaming too well on the long grade but some good work with the fire-irons soon had her boiling merrily again as at 11.30 we rolled into Five Rivers.

The Ab class has a 440-ton rating up to Eyre Creek, the next station from Five Rivers, but having dropped another wagon off at Five Rivers, it was doubtful whether the tonnage was even 40 that the old Ab was making so much fuss over. There is a steady grade up to Eyre Creek, but on the downgrade 784 raced away like a two-year-old filly instead of a 40-year-old shortly destined for the knacker's yards, her safety valves screaming from the force of escaping steam at over 180 lb to the square inch.

We stopped for lunch at the Athol Chapel (non-denominational) presided over by the resident priest, Harry, a surfaceman known the length and breadth of the Kingston line and even beyond. Harry was an unshaven, generously paunched, and affable host who invited us all, including the small boy, into the "Chapel", an indescribable confusion of jacks, picks, cans, crowbars, slashers, sacks, wire, shovels, and other tools of the surfaceman's trade. How his tool-hut ever came to be called the Chapel I have no idea, but it certainly was in keeping with Harry's reputation for being a character. The billy was boiled in the firebox and we all sat round to eat and pass the time of day. Besides its designation as a Chapel, Harry's hut also served as the local railway library and upon request he could produce from various sacks assorted paperback thrillers, Westerns, and other novels to be read and returned on the next trip up the branch.

From Athol the line climbs up through the hills past jutting outcrops of grey rock that pierce the tussock-covered slopes and the low front windows beside the boiler of an Ab gave an excellent view of the rough countryside through which the snorting engine made her way as the smoke of her passage rolled back over the countryside. At Garston, 1,009 feet high and 78 miles from town, where a little pub, a store and garage sit forlornly beside the highway, we dropped off the last empty wagon and reduced to the two loads for the S.S. *Earnslaw's* stokers. Over the small combined bridge on the dusty dirt road that meandered off to the hills rumbled the train, and the grade ahead steepened visibly until at 30 mph, as the cab crashed and shook, we bounced over the Fairlight Flats while the rumble of the Sellars injector I was working added to the general din. Finally, in country that with the slate-grey sky above and the brown hillsides with patches of blue lupins was beginning to resemble the Scottish Highlands, we drifted down the long bank and round the big curve into the little settlement of Kingston.

The engine was unhooked and clanked down to the pit, where

the fireman set to with the rake cleaning out his fire, leaving the glowing banks in the corners, but pushing the old clinker and ash over the drop grate in the centre of the box to fall into the pit. The firebars were considered too close and some skilful manoeuvring with the irons dropped two or three out into the pit while the rest were then spread to allow more draught into the box. Down to the turntable rumbled 784 and everyone strained and heaved as the old table slowly rotated to reverse the engine. When the water in the tender had been replenished and some shunting done, there was time to replenish the human element at a conveniently situated building set aside for the purpose, before heading back south.

Kingston now no longer has a station agent; the engine shed has gone, and only the turntable, pit, water tank and ganger's hut ever see much use these days, and that only two or three times a week.

The several small boys who had jammed the engine while we shunted, reluctantly dropped off and as the mist swept in from Lake Wakatipu we pulled slowly out of Kingston, the only freight aboard being a large Lake trout proudly held by the now triumphant lad headed back to Lumsden for a well-earned tea.

With only the van on her drawbar, the Ab's panting and thundering up the Kingston grade was the superb acting of an old trouper rather than any genuine effort, and she soon settled down for the mainly downhill run home again while I gave the fireman a spell with the firing. Apart from some shunting to pick up a few loaded wagons, some lost sweat on my part as I worked with the shovel, and a spirited horn-and-whistle exchange between the Ab and a beat-up Zephyr with much abusive hand signalling by the respective occupants of the mechanical sound duellists, the trip home was largely uneventful.

The warm glow of the heat from the backhead, the soft chuffing of the stack, and the quiet whisper of escaping steam created a cosy little cocoon of warmth and gentle sounds as the cold drizzle came on up the valleys to meet us and swept around the windows of the cab.

All too soon it was time to work the injector for the last time, throw in the last shovel of coal, and say farewell to 784, her friendly crew, and to Southland, where the traditions of steam and friendly hospitality are still to be found in very generous measure.

15

Where diesels fear to tread

THE WILD WEST COAST! Locale of a thousand legends, uncounted tall tales of men who are men and drink straight from kegs, where the mosquitoes are bigger than dragon-flies; where the coal is mined and the timber felled, and steam in all its pristine splendour reigns supreme. Where the only diesels in the whole region are three Ds shunters and a Tr yard tractor that keep a wary distance from the aggressive Ww and Wf engines also working the shunt. Haunt of the last of the narrow firebox We, Valhalla of the A and Ab and where the hearty echo of a J crashes around the hills. To the diesel-besotted fan from the "outland", the 18-stall roundhouse at Greymouth still provides a safe haven from the enveloping diesel fumes. The railways are not the least of the Coast's many claims that vest it almost with the status of a separate country.

Without doubt to my mind the most fascinating locomotive depot in the country, now that Cross Creek has gone, is the great American-styled roundhouse at Greymouth. To suddenly come upon the sight of a central turntable with tracks radiating off to the numbered stalls is to be instantly transported to pure Americana and the sights and sounds of the old-time steam round-house.

With the demise of the ramshackle wooden fixture at Invercar-gill, now replaced by a modern conventional shed, Greymouth has the only steam depot of its kind in the country. It is a magnificently equipped affair. Fine workshops which used to turn their own wheels carry out extensive repairs, necessitating the use of Hillside shops only for major overhauls.

The use of an automatic coal tipple makes the otherwise laborious task of coaling a matter of minutes. Coal hoppers are run over the pit and emptied, and the endless bucket chain lifts the coal up to the bins high in the massive concrete structure. It is the easiest of tasks to run the tender underneath the chute, wind the chain that controls the outlet, and shut it moments later with a full bunker of good Coast coal all ready for the firebox. There is no shovelling out of ashpits at Greymouth either. Another bucket chain conveys the ash and clinker straight to a waiting wagon. Greymouth is the supreme illustration that, given modern up-to-date facilities, steam locomotive servicing need not be a long, tedious chore. The only complaint crews have is the necessity of using the turntable every time an engine goes out into the yards.

"Old steamers never die, they simply gravitate to the West Coast," might well be the Coast railwayman's philosophy.

The profusion of antique locomotives at Greymouth has long been a legend among steam enthusiasts. Until recent years such vintage types as F, Ub, Uc, W and Wa classes were all working on the Coast in happy ignorance of the fact that most or all of their sister engines had long since vanished off the rest of the NZR tracks. The Ub and Uc 4-6-0 engines hardly needed whistles as they knocked and banged their way along with mixed trains in tow. The Greymouth crews were frequently bitter in their denunciation of engines they were still working through the 1950s. In the face of posters proclaiming "Protect your eyes", Wa289 wheezed along without bunker windows, and the fireman had to work with his eyes shut in a cloud of Wallsend coaldust.

"Discard worn-out tools" blared another poster. Ub330½ as she was named by Coast crews, a combination of the engine of 330 and tender of 331, broke in two on one occasion when the engine-tender coupling gave way and the frame was found to be rotten. The Uc engines, hated machines with their combination of large cylinders, short boilers and narrow fireboxes, had little in reserve even when in good order and frequently set forth from Stillwater with up to 70-total trains.

The W and Wa also came in for their share of abuse as they finished their days on the Coast. With their saturated boilers, bad valves, cramped cabs and old age they were sorry engines when they finally retired. W238, on one memorable occasion, left Greymouth, and while the crew were having their fifth boil-up (the engine, not the tea billy) at Brunner, eight miles out, the engine ran out of water. The crew cut off from the train and shot through to Stillwater three miles away to take water, returning then to their train to set about getting enough steam to move the train as well as the engine. A mile further on and the little W ran out of coal. There was no help for it: once more to Stillwater to rob a wagon, and back once more the hapless crew went, cursing their engine all the way until eventually they were able to move off in some semblance of regulation running.

In 1955 Greymouth was still receiving, as "new" engines, Wf and A classes, built respectively in 1904 and 1906-14. The 1904 vintage Wf383 is still working a daily shunt 62 years after she first rolled from the shops. The We class tank engines were rebuilt from B class engines of nineteenth-century vintage, and 375 still heads trains up to Rewanui. The first Ab, 804, arrived at Greymouth in 1956, at a time when the Abs had ceased intensive work on many North Island sections. The newest engines on the Coast are the J class locomotives formerly used in the Waikato and built by the North British Locomotive Works in 1939.

The amazing thing about it all, though, is that in a part of the country that probably relies more on the railways for moving goods and passengers than anywhere else in the whole of New Zealand, these generally very well maintained old girls perform prodigies of haulage with an incredible reliability. Greymouth is the supreme New Zealand example of the undeniable fact that given proper care, the life of the steam locomotive is virtually infinite.

The Coast can offer some superb trips, preferably on one of the several mixed trains that run daily to Ross, Otira, and Rewanui. Train 823, the early morning mixed train I rode to Ross and drove back, was somewhat of a holiday special. Normally there is no mixed service from Greymouth to Hokitika, the train becoming a mixed at Hokitika, going down to Ross and back to Greymouth still as a mixed as Train(s) 832/836.

The white haziness of Mount Cook was clear on the horizon as we left Greymouth aboard Ab823 with 300 tons of mixed freight in tow and the summer sun was eloquent testimony to the fact that tales of the Coast's rainy climate are exaggerated. The trip was slow and pleasant, and a stop of lengthy duration at Kumara on the return trip gave the opportunity to inspect both railway and the Railway Hotel premises in suitable fashion, a welcome relief from the coaldust and heat of the cab and the bright hot sunshine.

A trip in the old car of 836 can be just as pleasant an experience, and on a warm day it is cooler than the cab. The run up from Ross to Hokitika is a delightful one through unspoiled bush and cool green swamps; the only sound is of birds and the unhurried beat of the Ab's exhaust. At 4.15 p.m. the train clatters slowly out of Hokitika at a steady 15 mph. The old car is very old indeed. The ceiling, once white, has long ago turned to a dirty creamy-yellow, the seats have the odd carefully-mended tear, and the stained wood panelling represents a proud but bygone day in the coachbuilder's trade. Old it may have been, but the carriage was scrupulously clean. Soon the car was literally bouncing as at 30 mph it bobbed along while the smoke drifted past the windows.

According to the Coast railwaymen, the Department still runs "Mystery Trains", because on some of the old cars, no matter how hard the passenger peers out, it's still a mystery where he is headed for with so much dirt over the windows. I was pleasantly surprised that these sour comments appeared completely unfounded. On the day I rode in the car however it was mist and rain that did much to obscure the view, unfortunately a different day from my footplate trip on the same train.

The train ambled on through Chesterfield at almost a walking pace, not through any fault of the 50-year-old Ab up front, but in the absence of shunts on this day the train had 2 hours 28 minutes in which to cover the 25 miles to Greymouth. Railways on the Coast are generally less urgent, less hurried; they still perform a social function rather than a hidebound, strict-accounting, economic one, and therein lies much of the charm of an unhurried saunter through bush and valley with a 50-, or 60- or even 70-year-old steam engine puffing industriously away up front. Now came the hard slog up the Serpentine, a long grade with a series of reverse curves that made the old Ab stagger dramatically as she tackled the long exhausting stretch, until at 5 p.m. she plodded wearily into Kumara to wait an hour for the southbound mixed and northbound railcar to arrive.

Kumara bore an ominous sign on its goods shed: "Di engine limit". The diesels, like the Campbells, were obviously coming, though when is still fortunately uncertain. After an hour's wait, while misty rain splattered on the windows, like a spectre on the moors a headlight suddenly loomed up out of the mist and Train 835, the daily afternoon southbound mixed headed by Ab722, announced its presence with a whistle blast. The black boiler of the Ab slid out of the thick white curtain while her own black exhaust smoke mingled with the white as she nosed her way on to the second loop.

Shortly after, the sound of a horn blaring at the crossing announced the arrival of the railcar. After a decent interval, the Ab on our train blew a lusty blast and creaked down the outside loop, on to the main loop and out on to the main line again, to churn softly off into the all-enveloping mist. Through more bush

Loafing through the Wairarapa Valley in a scene reminiscent of all the now-vanished provincial expresses, is Ab755 at the head of the Up Wairarapa Mail crossing the old Waiohine Bridge.

Steam Defiant! The exhaust is bellowing as smoke pours into the air, Ja1270 charges out of Christchurch with the Southbound Limited. The author fired this engine at 70 mph on the run north from Timaru.

Top: Ja1270, on which the author rode to Christchurch, receives attention to her running gear while taking water at Timaru before heading the South Island Limited north.

Centre: Almost obscured in a self-created fog, an Ab shunting in the Palmerston North yards seems determined to try to hide a sister Ab quietly awaiting an assignment.

Bottom: Increasing wage-bills and decreasing labour meant that the bright green, highly polished brassbound engines of better days gave way to black and soot. But K912 at Wanganui in April 1964 proved that even modern engines do get cleaned on very rare occasions.

rumbled the train while ferns brushed caressing fronds along the blush-red car sides until at 6.38 the train trundled unhurriedly into the Greymouth Station.

There are still two mixed trains each way morning and afternoon between Greymouth and Otira, in addition to the railcar services, and a late shopping-night-cum-picture train departs from Greymouth still at 10.31 p.m. on Fridays. Train 780, the afternoon mixed up to Otira, gives a leisurely run through the hills and valleys of the Coast on the beautiful trip up to the mountains. The day I travelled saw J1208 with a puny train of about 100 tons total, a van coupled to the engine, the inevitable old wooden car, and trailing this a rake of empty M open wagons.

It was obvious that only regulars normally travelled on the train. The guard, a cheerfully gregarious fellow, clipped my ticket and said: "What the hell are you travelling on *this* for? Why not wait and go up on the railcar?" I hastened to explain that I was in fact travelling for the sheer pleasure of sampling steam mixed train travel. His reply was typical of the true Coaster. "Well for God's sake don't sit here then, come on up in the van with me."

Soon, ensconced in the decrepit van, I was watching the bush slide by as the J did her best to hold herself in check with her light train. Normally 780 is a full 420-ton train up the heavily graded line and the fireman may shift four or more tons of coal in the 52-mile run when the coal wagons are dragging on the drawbar. At Moana, thanks to fellows as hospitable as one could wish to meet, I was invited to join the crew on the footplate. It was to a certain extent a stroke of luck for the driver that he asked me up, because while lifting the heavy hose on the water-vat, the fireman strained some back muscles and, groaning in agony, had to be assisted off the tender. It was obvious that the poor fellow was in no condition to shovel coal, and the driver, normally employed on the sedentary position of a railcar driver, was clearly concerned at the thought that he might have to get even this light train up to Otira singlehanded.

With a seeming casualness I mentioned that by this time I was not a complete novice with a coal shovel, hoping desperately that I did indeed look an old hand at this sort of thing. The fireman allowed that he could probably do the driving without further damaging himself, and so it was that with a crew consisting of a partially disabled fireman in the driver's seat, an experienced but long-out-of-firing-practice driver, and a relatively inexperienced but recently-in-firing-practice enthusiast, taking turns at the shovel and injectors, that J1208 plugged her way off up the line to Otira.

K

We certainly had some fun. The fireman would wince every time he moved the regulator or cut-off lever. The driver and I took sweating turns on the shovel, usually indicated by such phrases as "Right, you have a go Dave, I've had it", or "I don't think that last lot caught properly, I'd hate to clog her, you better do the next lot!" Even with a light train the firing was hot and heavy sweating work. I hate to think what it might have been like with 400 tons pulling on the tender.

The track was pretty rough in places and the J tended not so much to ride it as fight it, which resulted in some fairly heavy riding for some miles. It was still a very pleasant trip though, as the late afternoon sun lit up the hills, obscured only by the rolling billows of the smoke from the two-man-fed fire. After Roto Manu, reached at 6.15, there is some flat running and the J was shaking along in great style for several miles. At Inchbonnie we stopped while the guard and a bearded hunter loaded two deer and a pig carcase into the van for the wild-meat agents. The fireman's venison steak tea was meanwhile cooking nicely in a greaseproof paper packet up on the boiler.

At Jacksons we banked the fire up well for the worst part of the run, the 11 miles of 1 in 66 grade to Otira, and from then on there was some solid shovel work required. The injector was working almost constantly, and a train that has not at least a three-quarter-full boiler at Aickens, five miles from Otira, stands very little chance indeed of making those last few miles. Finally we crested the last of the grade into Otira, where the number of people not employed on the Railways can be counted on one hand, and left J1208 for the shed crew to pick up. It had certainly been an interesting trip, and for me a particularly satisfying one, where my efforts with the shovel had for once been more than a mere kindly indulgence on the part of the crew. It seemed a fitting note upon which to end what was my final footplate trip on a Coast steamer.

There are perhaps few railway lines quite so intriguing as bush tramways, with their rickety track, often very narrow gauges, and their quaint engines like refugees from Emmett cartoons, and nowhere in New Zealand has there been such a profusion of bush tramways as on the West Coast. A glance at a railway map of the Coast gives the impression that it's had a tin of spaghetti emptied over it – the weaving lines run in all directions among the thick bush.

Today, the only steam bush line left is the New Forest Sawmilling Company's line at Ngahere. It is a pale shadow, a mere one-mile siding from the Westport main line to the mill, of the network of line over which the Heisler-geared engines once wheezed their smoky way through the bush, trailing wagons with the great logs on their way to the mill. Today a Heisler can still be seen clanking its way around the mill sidings, while another sits in reserve with its universals greased ready to be fired up as necessary; but the end cannot be much longer away.

At Ogilvie's Gladstone mill two bush engines sit rusting while a tractor shunts wagons in the yard. A diesel bush railcar still moves gear around on the odd occasion, but the line that it once traversed with men for the bush, is now only a curving bank along a river bed where it disappears up into the forest. All over the Coast you can still find the abandoned remains of old lines. Near the gold dredge workings on the Taramakau River is one such mill.

The mill is like the *Marie Celeste* – it appears simply to have been abandoned en masse or its workers uprooted by some unnatural agency. Narrow-gauge light iron tracks cut around the yard where the remains of trolleys lie rusting. Wider gauge "main line" tracks run off over a trestle bridge that spans a stream, and the formation curves around a tiny valley, literally only feet wide, that meanders back into the bush. An old McCormick-Deering tractor, fixed to a flat wagon with drive shafts to where twin driving bogies were mounted, sits high and dry on blocks. The crumbling remains of an old Model A Ford bus lie in ruins in the blackberry. It is enough to make any railway historian scream in frustration at the crumbling track and vehicles now lost for ever to posterity.

The mill itself is in good order. Stacks of beautifully weathered timber lie all over the yard. A perfectly good steam generator that used to drive the belts connected to the saws sits in an open shed awaiting the fire in its grate that is unlikely ever again to be kindled. Piles of rusting tramway rails lie stacked neatly in the open. The remains of a wooden-railed line run off in another direction. The mill lies abandoned in the summer sun and winter rain, a spot rich in history, where the sweat of men and the force of steam converted great logs into orderly piles of timber. Lost, abandoned, forgotten, a still practically complete example of one of the more romantic institutions in New Zealand's railway and national history waits for the inexorable bush and blackberry to hide it for ever from the eye of man. It is a forlorn, depressing sight.

The bush tramways may have gone, but the coalmines still depend upon the railway to move their products. Two famous mine branches are the Blackball and Rewanui Inclines. Blackball was opened in 1910 when the little W class engines struggled up to the bins at Blackball and Roa on the 1 in 25 grades to bring out the coal. In later years B class tender engines thrashed their way up, the fireman working like a madman to keep the narrow little firebox full. Regrettably the days of the Blackball line appear to have ended. In 1966 the bridge over the Grey River collapsed in a flood and it will not be replaced.

Fortunately, however, the other Incline line on the Coast, that up to Rewanui, is still functioning, though now without the centre-rail that the Fell brake vans used to grip on the 1 in 26 descent from the mine. Rewanui used to enjoy the distinction, not only of being a centre-rail line (although the rail was used only for braking, not climbing) but of providing the only access to the State mine perched high up in the mountain crags. But now the ugly brown scar of a road slashes through the bush, and Rewanui's distinctions now reside in its rugged scenic magnificence and the little tank engines that daily grind their way up the hill.

The centre-rail was still there, the line was the only access, and the bush unscarred when I climbed on to the footplate of Ww679 waiting on the wharf line at Greymouth at 6.15 a.m. on a summer day in 1965. The smoke rolled in a furious black cloud from the stack as the twin brake pumps banged regularly from the front of the engine. Ww679 had been known as "the fireman's enemy" when she was in service up at Gisborne, but the old girl seemed to have lost the worst of her ferocious appetite and the normal firing rate was ample for her on the flat. The train make-up was four empty Q hopper wagons; the Q is a New Zealand-designed coal wagon which can be swung clear of its chassis, out over the ship and the contents discharged directly into the hold. In addition were two La open wagons, the car, Fell van, and guard's van. At 6.35 a.m. the shrill piping of the Ww's English-sounding whistle screamed out over the river and we clattered down past the signal box where the fireman took the tablet that is located on a pulley strung over the tracks, and then the train slowly rattled out across the old wooden truss bridge over the eddying water of the river – reputedly the only S-bend railway bridge in the country.

The line turns through the bush-dotted slopes of the hills beside the river for a few chains and then the Ww gathered up her skirts and set off through the bush towards Runanga, while the smoke poured in a never-ending torrent from the funnel. The line passes through bush so luxuriant, cuttings so steep, that with the smoke wafting overhead it seemed like twilight in the cramped little cab.

At Runanga several miners boarded the train, but as the mine was closed for holidays, only maintenance crews were making the trip up. The La wagons are put to use, oddly enough, for bicycles. It is standard practice for the men to cycle back down the hill when their shift is over.

At Dunollie, a mile or two further on, more men joined the train and the car began to fill up. On the footplate the fireman was busy with his shovel, because just out of Dunollie the over-three-mile centre-rail climb up to the mine begins. At the foot of the incline the train stopped while the guard trudged forward to set the points from the runaway line to the main; then it inched forward, waited for the points again and the guard to board, and then began the heaving, grunting struggle that is the sound of a small steam engine hauling herself and a train up the 1 in 26 to 1 in 30 gradients to Rewanui. At the time of my trip there was an official 6 mph speed restriction but the standard practice of the crews was to give her her head and concentrate simply on getting up, the hell with what the speed happened to be.

With the sander hissing on and off, the regulator out and the cut-off right forward, 679 blasted and thundered her way up the valley, the beating exhaust notes crashing and echoing round the valley as smoke blasted up towards the shreds of mist hanging around the mountain tops like bodgies on a street corner. The engine jerked as the wheels slipped on greasy rail, the tortured exhaust was a trembling crescendo of sound throbbing through the bush as the sun's rays glinted on the green leaves of the damp trees.

On upwards the little engine laboured, past the private mines that stud the hillsides every so often, their cableways disappearing up the mountainsides. Round curves struggled the train, through tunnels like caves in the hillside as the unlined walls threw rocks into sharp relief and deep shadow when the headlight swept over them. The fireman plied his shovel while watching the boiler water-level carefully. The little Ww has a tendency to "prime" – that is, lift water and blow it out the exhaust, if the water is allowed to rise too high in the boiler. The Ww has a tendency to slip at the slightest provocation, unlike the heavier We, rated to pull 100 tons up the grade compared to the 85 of the Ww.

Bucking and slipping, the little engine inched her way up the final grade and as the exhaust went mad in a final frantic hulla-baloo of sound while the wheels spun on the last part of the grade, she staggered into the small, flat yard at Rewanui. The Q hoppers were shunted over a little bridge spanning a mountain stream, and left under the chutes of the massive coal bins on the other side. Other odd shunting chores were performed and then the engine scuttled thirstily along to the water-vat fed by the clear cool water of the stream. With the last drops of water dripping from her tank 679 prepared for the descent, marshalling her train so that the Fell van was in the centre. With another of the peeping little whistle-blasts, 679 eased her way, bunker first, out of the yard. Again there was a halt, for the runaway points to be set to the main line down the hill, and then the engine eased her train down the grade.

The run down the hill was easy, the brakes hissed off and on almost constantly, while in the Fell van the guard spun the brake wheel to help check the speed of the descending train. Now only the air brakes hold the train; the Fell rail and vans have finally followed their locomotive namesakes and been removed from the NZR. The run down is in marked contrast to the slog up, and it is not long before the train grinds to a halt at the foot of the hill to allow the points to be changed again. When I travelled on 679 it was also necessary to unwind the centre-rail brakes, because the immense pressure caused them to lock together if they were left on when the centre-rail terminated, necessitating a considerable amount of work by the fitters before they were operable again. At Dunollie and Runanga the train picks up office and shop workers on their way to Greymouth and a day's work, before the Ww takes up the slack for a brisk trot back through the bush to arrive at Greymouth again at 8.23 a.m.

The future of the Rewanui branch is assured. There is ample coal lying buried deep in the hillside. But the duration of the present motive power is uncertain. Only one We still remains, but the Ww tank engines are still much in evidence, though their days must surely be numbered. The road that now scars the once virgin bush on the opposite side of the valley was just the beginning of the end for Rewanui. The removal of the centre-rail was the middle stage, and when the tinny whistle of a Ww and the thrash-ing of her tortured exhaust and beating pistons no longer echo off the grey slate cliff faces on the climb to Rewanui then progress, and its attendant mediocrity, will have laid waste one of the last great stamping-grounds of King Steam.

16

The great motive power debate

IN THE LAST 20 YEARS argument has waxed long and furious
over the relative merits of steam, diesel, and electric traction.
At most gatherings of rail fans the apparently inexhaustible
debate goes on: "They shouldn't scrap engines in the prime of
their life." "Millions of pounds of overseas funds are being spent
on these ugly blasted things [diesels]." "We should have spent our
money on electrification." And so it goes on.

It is not only rail fans that debate the issue either. The controversy has still not been unanimously resolved by railway engineers
themselves, though engineers these days generally debate diesel *v.*
electric. As in any debate, neither side can score an overwhelming
win, there are points in favour and points against; but in view of
the considerable controversy among rail fans, some consideration
must be given to the debate to determine, if possible, how the
relative merits of each form of traction apply in New Zealand
conditions, and what the Railways are doing in respect of each.

With a few exceptions, steam is losing ground all over the world.
Its opponents decry it as a legacy of Victorian days, an inefficient,
expensive, and unsophisticated method of railway propulsion. It is
spurned as outmoded, unable to cope with modern traffic, and its
performance scathingly compared with that of the diesel. The
picture generally projected is of a sad, leaky, beat-up giant wheezing black fumes of noxious smoke, clanking off along the siding
to oblivion. But the final analysis of any locomotive type is a
mixture of several factors: its economics, its availability, and its
performance. For all its apparent complexity the modern steam
locomotive is essentially a simple mechanism, using principles that
have stood the test of time for well over a century. Refinements
have been made to improve performances, but in the essential
principles, the modern Ja is basically identical to Stephenson's
Rocket.

This principle, that of expanded steam being used in the

cylinders to move the pistons, then being turned up the chimney, creating a draught for the fire and pulling the hot gases and smoke through the boiler tubes, thereby providing heat additional to that of the firebox, has remained virtually unchanged over the years. Because of its essential simplicity there is less to go wrong with a steam locomotive which has far less moving parts than a diesel engine. Steam power is, provided it receives normal maintenance, extremely reliable; failures are infrequent and are usually the result of reciprocating parts, the pistons, side rods or valves packing up.

An advantage, or disadvantage, depending upon which side of the fence one sits, is the "inner reserve" of most steam engines. With diesel or electric traction, the ultimate in power to be expected from a particular engine can be exactly computed because the power output is almost constant at given speeds over the whole of a particular class. Like animals though, steam locomotives can vary considerably within a class. Certain Kas were regularly assigned to express work because they were "better pullers" or "good steamers", yet to all outward appearances two engines would be identical. When driven by a man who knows his engine and with a fireman skilled in his trade, steam engines can be worked well past their designed limits by skilful driving and constant firing. Conversely however this also means that with a less skilled crew the steam locomotive will not respond as efficiently, the result being perhaps excessive fuel consumption and unnecessary strain on the moving parts. By comparison, the other forms of traction do not have this disadvantage and a mediocre driver may work a train as well as a more skilled and able man. The diesel or electric locomotive is far less dependent upon the skill of its crew for efficient performance.

The basic disadvantage of the steam locomotive is its acknowledged thermal inefficiency. The use of exhaust steam to provide draught for the fire is steam wasted, and the gases being forced out of the smokebox by the draught necessary to maintain a hot fire are lost into the atmosphere before they have exhausted a very great proportion of their heat. Overall, the thermal efficiency of the modern steam engine is not much above 8 per cent.

Servicing is the other main disability suffered by steam power. The firebox must be regularly raked and clinker and ash dropped. The engine must stop for water at intervals and, unless further time is to be lost, engines must be changed when fuelling (coal or oil) becomes necessary. About the turn of this century, various experiments were begun to try to improve the efficiency of the steam locomotive, efforts which were intensified as the threat from diesel manufacturers gathered momentum. Such measures included compounding, where high-pressure steam, having worked a normal set of cylinders, instead of being released into the atmosphere passed into a second, low-pressure, set of cylinders. Many of the American articulated locomotives worked on this principle. The New Zealand A class locomotives started as compounds, but as with many other compound engines, difficulties in their maintenance outweighed the advantage of the double use of steam.

Efforts were directed towards other developments in the field of high-pressure steam, the idea being to make the greatest use of the expansive properties of steam thereby conserving fuel and water. Steam turbine units were also developed by various designers, substituting the steam turbine for cylinders and reciprocating motion. These designs had the advantage of eliminating the hammer-blow when the wheels, which must be balanced against the motion of the rods and pistons (usually up to two-thirds), revolve at a greater speed than they are balanced for, and in extreme cases are lifted clear of the track at each revolution. The effect on the track of 145 tons of locomotive doing this can well be imagined.

Steam turbines were, however, despite early isolated efforts, a last-ditch experiment, and dieselisation overcame them before any real evaluation of their future could be made. Monsters like the Norfolk and Western Railroad's No 2300 "Jawn Henry", despite 30 per cent greater thermal efficiency than reciprocating steam locomotives, and up to 144,000 lb tractive effort, were built too late to turn the tide and were scrapped in most cases after a working life of only a few years.

With very few exceptions, notably India, China, Cuba, South Africa, and the Argentine, most countries in the world now build or buy only diesel or electric locomotives. In Europe, where electricity is cheap, electric traction is being most rapidly developed as the prime mover but steam continues to be used as the secondary power, and many European countries have fine studs of steamers. Where oil is cheap, as in the USA, diesel power stands supreme in the foreseeable future. The great advantage both these forms of power have is their availability. An engine is only of use when it is out on the road pulling trains and earning revenue for its owner. In theory diesel and electric units are available for longer periods because their servicing requirements are less and servicing is not required as frequently.

Diesel traction is extremely flexible, and can go wherever there are rails, as compared with electricity, which must of course, rely on energy generated outside the body of the locomotive. The diesels and electrics as compared with steam, can pack great power inside a smaller and less weighty locomotive. While the diesel locomotive has not yet been built that could as a single unit out-haul some of the massive steam locomotives built in America, (the Duluth, Missabe and Iron Range articulateds regularly pulled 20,000 tons trailing iron-ore trains), the great weight of a steam locomotive and tender necessary for increased power, must always be related to the track and loading gauge of the system it runs over.

The ultimate in railway traction is universally recognised as electricity. Almost without exception, electric traction can fairly lay claim to being the most efficient form of railway locomotion. It has practically unlimited possibilities. Deriving energy from an outside source, electric units can deliver much more power than alternative modes of traction of comparable weight and dimension. The abounding advantages of electric traction are offset only by the initial high cost of its installation.

An American engineer, Thomas Martin, made an intensive study of the relative merits of diesel and electric traction in the United States, and the paper he published gives some highly interesting figures by way of comparison between the two types of power. He examined the cost of locomotive running repairs between the two modes and found that on an equated tractive effort basis, the cost of maintaining a diesel locomotive was twice that of a straight electric. He found that although in America in 1947, the cost of dieselising at 60 million US dollars was half that of electrification, assuming identical traffic patterns, the electrified portions would have saved 7·5 million dollars per annum on operating expenses, and the additional cost of electrification would have been amortised in about eight years.

He also found that by means of a graph showing tractive effort versus speed characteristics of the two types of locomotives of equal gross weight with all axles powered, taking a 1 in 50 com-pensated ruling grade 20 miles long at 30 mph, four electric loco-motives would handle 3,090 tons trailing as against 2,910 tons for six diesel locomotives. His figures using the amount of tons trailed per ton of locomotive, showed that electrics were 58 per cent more efficient.

Martin's argument is that with fewer locomotives needed for the same work, the capital costs of motive power thus offset can be applied to the capital costs of catenary construction. It can also be reasonably expected that the average working life of an electric locomotive will be longer than that of a diesel locomotive.

The electrification of the Main Trunk, long a favourite hobby horse for many, was thoroughly investigated between 1948 and 1951, and the conclusion reached that at that time it was not economically justified. Electrification could doubtless do much to further speed up workings. Electrics could cope even more efficiently with this difficult section of railway than the present diesels are doing. Perhaps in time electrification may come, and there have been learned engineers who felt that it should. At the present time, however, the Das are coping very well with freight traffic (subject to doubts expressed later on their passenger haulage performances) and it appears most unlikely that further electrification in New Zealand could be justified for some time to come.

New Zealand is now committed to total dieselisation, and in the North Island this has been practically completed; only isolated pockets of steam remain until the further diesels now on order will replace them. By 1970, on present estimates, steam power in New Zealand will be no more. This is a momentous change, and despite the feelings of emotion that the change arouses in many people, it cannot be charged that the Railways Department rushed into it with quite the same indecent haste as happened in the USA. The question may fairly be asked however: "Are we doing the right thing?" As previously stated, the whole question must of course be decided on economic grounds.

The capital outlay is one very important factor. A diesel unit costs on the average at least twice as much as a steam locomotive of equivalent power, which can and generally has been built in New Zealand with the greatest success. By contrast, immense loans are now being raised with the World Bank to finance New Zealand's suddenly increased dieselisation programme. As a general rule of thumb it is also accepted that the life of a diesel locomotive is roughly half that of a steam engine. This has been found overseas, where the economic life of a diesel locomotive is generally accepted as being 15 to 20 years. In the United States most Class I railroads now operate second-generation diesels, replacing units purchased during or after the Second World War.

The initial high cost and shorter life of the diesels are two vital factors. The diesels' availability for almost continuous service is essential if they are to be economic from a capital point of view. As an illustration, if a steam locomotive costs, say $80,000 and has a service life of 30 years, the annual average of capital investment cost spread over such period is $2,666. A diesel locomotive costing say $160,000, and having a service life of 15 years, averages its capital investment cost at $10,666 per annum; or, spread over a period of 20 years, which seems to be the diesels' maximum main line life expectancy, averages at $8,000 per year. The diesels' economy can therefore, very rapidly become a liability if maximum utilisation is not exercised. In the light of such illustrations it can readily be appreciated that an apparently miraculous availability for service on the part of the diesel is nothing more than economic necessity, and that if such utilisation is not made, the advantages of diesel over steam become economically nebulous on a capital investment basis.

Against this argument is to be balanced the undeniable fact that in New Zealand the diesel is a cheaper locomotive to operate. The average fuel consumption of a Da or Df diesel-electric locomotive on a run from Wellington to Auckland is $1\frac{1}{3}$ gallons per mile. With a comparable load a Ka would use about seven gallons of fuel oil per mile, and require several refuelling stops, whereas the Da is able to make a non-stop run. Diesel fuel costs almost twice as much per gallon as fuel oil, but the lessened consumption provides the favourable economic result for the diesel. It has been stated, and there seems no reason to doubt, that two Das can take twice the load in half the time that a Ka is able to. But this type of statement can be misleading; after all, two modern locomotives of equivalent or greater power *ought* to be able to shift twice as much in a shorter time than one engine of a class designed over a quarter of a century ago, themselves a development of a design now over 36 years old. Many sweeping claims have been made concerning the diesel's superior capacity, all of which fail to take into account the fact that they are being compared with steam engines nearing the end of their economic life and having only the minimum of attention given to them.

Incredible as their performances were over their life-span, it must be admitted that most of the North Island steam engines were nearing the end of their tether, and replacement was clearly necessary. The retirement of the fine, modern, oilburning Jas in the Auckland district can be justified only on the grounds (economically sound) that it is an unwarranted expense to maintain separate facilities for both steam and diesel.

The merits of dieselisation of the South Island by 1970 may well be questioned. The South Island has large supplies of coal readily available, and excellent steaming coal it is too. It has a good stock of modern Ja class locomotives equipped with most of the modern devices available to steam engineers. In addition to the native Jas, a number of Abs and Js in good order have been shipped south to replace many of the more antiquated steam locomotives formerly in use. Some of the Jas are of even more recent construction than the North Island Das. By 1970 they will be only 14 or 15 years old, mere youngsters, as steam engines go. And yet they are slated to be replaced by diesels. There may be sound economic reasons for this, but they have not generally been made public and are hard for the layman to readily discern. In addition it is understood that one of the conditions of the World Bank loan was that dieselisation should be speeded up. Why this should be a condition is difficult to understand.

An article in the *New Zealand Mercantile Gazette* referring to the Railways loans, stated recently: "When we raise loans let it not be at the behest and for the benefit of Standard Oil and General Motors." This may or may not be fair comment, but it certainly provides one explanation of such an unusual condition for a loan when the Railways already have *modern* motive power in the South Island, even if it is steam.

That dieselisation must come in the South Island is inescapable. The trend cannot be reversed now, but whether it should be pursued in such haste seems doubtful. The steam engines may cost more to run, but this has to be measured against the millions of dollars being tied up in their replacements. It is unfortunate also that diesel units of greater power are not being utilised. The Di class will have a rating of 580 tons up to Arthur's Pass as compared with the 26-year-old Kb's 600 tons. In order to haul more loads, two locomotives will be necessary, and the cost of two low-powered units is generally greater than the cost of one higher powered unit. Mr T. C. Pant, Joint Director (Diesel) of the Ministry of Railways Research Designs and Standards Organisation, India, in a study on the "Evolution of Broad Gauge Freight Locomotives in India" states:

Notwithstanding that multiple operation of diesel and electric locomotives involves no additional cost on staff, it is basically uneconomic and inelegant to use two locomotives for duties which can perhaps be performed by one. Functional efficiency and economy demands minimisation of the necessity for multiple working, and today the evolution of diesel and electric locos is directed towards this objective.

It appears inevitable that on present traffic trends and motive power available, New Zealand will be forced to rely heavily on multiple-unit working.

The lack of higher-powered locomotives is also apparent on the Limited schedules in the North Island, where the use of Das has resulted in a net reduction of only 45 minutes on the schedule previously maintained by steam engines. This change is due in large part to the elimination of time wasted on water stops and engine changes, and not to any increase in the overall speed of the train. It can only be assumed that the Da is incapable of handling the Limited at any greater speeds over the difficult Main Trunk. Diesels of (say) 2,000 hp should have little difficulty in bettering the present schedule, and possibly in the future, electrification may have the chance to prove its tremendous potential for the speeding up of trains.

Indeed it is to electrification that South Africa, wherever possible, is turning rather than to diesel traction. South Africa has a large (2,500) stud of the finest steam locomotives that run on 3 foot 6 inch gauge, the latest of which were placed in service in 1953-5. Because all diesel fuel must be imported, whereas adequate supplies of coal exist (which is basically the situation in this country) South Africa, wherever traffic is heavy enough to warrant it, uses electricity. Diesel traction is at present very much third best and is used only where traffic is light and water scarce. On other lines the fine GO and GMA/M Garratts and the superb Class 25 and 25 NC 4-8-2 engines handle all the workings and they will continue to do so for as long as economically possible and until then will be used to the maximum possible extent. New steam locomotives, Garratts, are now on order for the 2-foot gauge South African lines. It may well be argued that South Africa's policy of conservation of steam locomotives for as long as possible is a policy that should be considered for the South Island, at the very least for Southland and the West Coast, which have extensive coalfields in their areas.

And so the great motive power debate continues, with railway engineers confident that they have made the right choice and committed to pursuing their stated policy of dieselisation with even greater speed.

Quoting increased revenues and operating profits, utilising the diesels for many more hours a day than steam locomotives could operate, running long non-stop trains, the Railway management are confident of the economic soundness of their policies. At the other extreme and of no importance, are the unabashed sentimentalists, whose arguments are emotional rather than economic, whose criterion is: "If it steams then it must be all right, nothing that uses diesel fuel can ever be any good."

In the middle are those like myself who recognise that the diesel has many advantages over much of our present steam power, but are not convinced that steam power in any form is *prima facie* uneconomic or inferior to diesel power. While diesel power has effected economies in running costs, it is the increased tonnage hauled that has given the Railways most of their operating profits. The Railways have lost money some years, and all the diesels in the world could not have prevented such loss in the face of declining traffic. Food for thought is provided by an American engineer, H. F. Brown, in a paper read to the Institution of Mechanical Engineers, London, wherein he came to the conclusion that diesel power had increased the financial burden of the American railroads, and that all in all, the diesel locomotive's economic performance was on about a par with that of steam, no better and no worse. In the explosive world situation today there is also the sobering consideration that if there were any large-scale conflict New Zealand's railways would be relying entirely upon imported fuels.

These sharply conflicting points of view, as in any debate, tend to confuse and bewilder the objective observer, who is faced with conflicting economic arguments, each based upon its own sound reasoning. As indicated by its title, this chapter is a debate, and I have endeavoured to present each case fairly, while at the same time putting forward some conclusions of my own on this absorbing discussion. The New Zealand Railways are now committed to total elimination of steam in the shortest possible time.

While in no way trying to argue that steam should be permanently retained, I am not yet convinced that the present *rapid* total dieselisation policy is necessarily the best and, along with many others interested in the New Zealand Railways I shall watch with interest the eventual operating and economic outcome of the Railways policy. Only time will tell which course is economically the better.

17

Passenger trains

I**T IS A FAIRLY FASHIONABLE** New Zealand pastime to indulge in the popular parlour game of "Slanging the Railways". The participants are required to speak for a minimum of five minutes about the time that Aunt Martha's suitcase was sent to the wrong station, or how the furniture was battered in transit, or how slow the last train trip was. The player winning the most points though is the one who can hold forth longest on the subject of the passenger trains. It is probable that Aunt Martha's case went to the wrong station because she omitted to label it, and the furniture may well have been bumped by the carrier who unloaded the wagon, but the fact remains that there is indeed a kernel of truth in aspersions cast on the passenger train. There is no doubt that despite the tremendous technical advances and changes the New Zealand Railways have made, particularly in the last few years, with new wagons, diesels, signalling, and many other improvements, the much-maligned express train has benefited by very few of them.

Railway travel in the early days however could give rise to even more justifiable complaint. The little old four- and six-wheeled English vehicles which replaced open goods wagons were hard riding, cold and uncomfortable, with wooden bench seating longitudinally fixed along each side of the carriage. There was no form of heating whatsoever and flickering colza oil lamps lit the narrow little interior. The late A. P. Godber, one of New Zealand's earliest railway enthusiasts, recorded that passengers were known to make bets as to which lamp was alight in the compartment of the carriage, and matches would then be struck to decide whether the lamp was lit or not. A gradual improvement commenced with the introduction of American Pullman vehicles in 1879 for use on the Christchurch-Dunedin expresses. The cars featured chair seats and toilets for the first time in New Zealand, as well as being the first bogie-wheeled passenger vehicles to run on the New Zealand Rail-

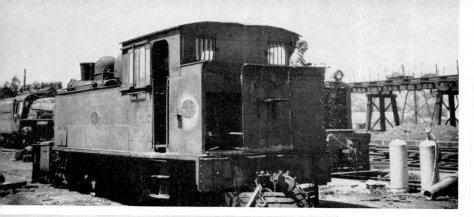

Centre: Enough to reduce any enthusiast to tears is the sight of once-proud K926 sitting broken and useless on a riverside scrap track at Wanganui, one of the great graveyards of North Island steamers.

Top: The end of the road. In a scene symbolic of Steam's last days an old Wf suffers the indignity of the torch; on the nearby track can be seen the front of her diesel replacement on the shunt.

Bottom: Quietly resting beside the Taumarunui Station sits Wa386, the engine that hauled the first train, the Parliamentary Special, over the last section of the Main Trunk in 1908.

Top: It's a hot day at Taihape and Ka930, the first of her class, is taking it easy. The driver relaxes, the engine simmers quietly, as man and machine relax before their next assignment.

Bottom: "Preservation" such as this makes the enthusiast doubt the worth of leaving little A class *Opossum* to waste away. She sits rotting beside the main line at Greymouth, little more than junk.

ways. Average speed on the early expresses was only 15-20 mph and the maximum permitted speed was 30 mph. Whatever short-comings they may still have, the New Zealand passenger trains of today are worlds removed from their ancestors.

The standard passenger vehicle of the New Zealand Railways today is the 56-foot-long steel-panelled vehicle seen on all main express trains, arranged either as 56-seat second-class cars, 31-seat first-class or, in the South Island, 29 first-class seats and a six-seat private compartment. The second-class cars are reasonably comfortable at the fares charged and for a short journey only are adequate enough. The first-class cars with their four-position reclining seats give a good standard of day accommodation, again at a reasonable fare. They are even tolerable enough for the reasonably physically fit, on the long overnight journey between Wellington and Auckland. The sleeping-cars in use again provide a reasonable standard, but two must share the rather confined compartment, which makes them a drawback to many.

The main problem is not that the cars *are* at least 20 years old, but that a great many of them *look* even older. The first-class car's reclining seats, footrests, pull-down rack for book or cup, hot and cold washbasins, make for quite comfortable travel. It is the décor that leaves so much to be desired. The old dark red, almost brown, leather of the seats is often scuffed and knocked around and gives at times the general effect of a dingy Victorian parlour. The seats in fact are a good deal more comfortable than those in, say, a Friendship aircraft, but the poor old brown leather comes off a very poor psychological second-best. By contrast, at least two cars in use on the South Island Limited are attractively furnished with seats in two shades of light blue, giving the whole car a clean, airy, cheerful appearance in strong contrast with the remainder of the train.

The old days when trains were the only method of travelling from Auckland to Wellington or Dunedin to Christchurch have long gone, but there has been little vigorous movement made to enable the railways to effectively meet their competitors. The main advantages of rail travel are (or should be) comfort, safety, relaxation, moderate fares, reasonable speed, and an opportunity to take in the scenery if desired. In the face of competition from modern turbo-prop, and soon jet, aircraft, and modern buses, the railways can only offer 20-year-old rolling-stock with the minimum of trappings and, despite new diesel locomotives, schedules that are frequently tediously slow.

The introduction of diesel locomotives on the Night Limited

L

and Express has done nothing except reduce the time allowed for servicing and changing steam engines, a matter of some 45 minutes. This in itself is not fatal provided that the passenger spends the time in attractive surroundings, which are generally lacking at the moment. The recently retired General Manager of the Railways, Mr A. T. Gandell, who has done much to improve the system, stated in an interview with the *Auckland Star* in October 1966, shortly before his retirement: "On the passenger side I have had some regrets that more has not been done. But in a modernisation programme, it's essential to sort out the priorities and stick to them. Freight revenue has doubled in the last 30 years; passenger traffic has been almost stationary in the last 15 years. Revenue from passengers is only 7 per cent of our gross revenue."

This is all perfectly true but it does seem to omit or at least pass over several factors. The railways have, while by no stretch of the imagination a monopoly, a very definite advantage in the movement of freight. This is inherent in the very principle of a train. They do not however have anything faintly resembling a monopoly in passenger traffic, except perhaps in the Wellington suburban area, and no real effort has been made to compete with other forms of passenger transport on such routes as the Auckland-Wellington run. It also would appear more than probable that passenger traffic has remained stationary simply because there has been so little done to improve the facilities on express trains to the point where they can reasonably compete for the passenger who now travels by plane or bus.

It is a crushing indictment that in 1965, whereas nine million people made long-distance trips by Railways Road Services buses, only 2·8 million made long-distance railway trips − and this includes the generally popular railcars. An unfortunate impression is given of putting the cart before the horse: "Until more people ride on the trains why improve them," rather than "Let's improve them and more people will ride on trains," seems to be the impression given by the Department and it is a singularly unfortunate one.

Some three years ago it was announced that work on modern stainless-steel trains on the latest overseas patterns was to be undertaken with a view to providing up-to-date facilities for long-distance travellers on the Main Trunk. At present, consideration is being given to the design of roomette and twinette sleeping accommodation and it is certainly to be hoped that the estimated further three to four years given as the earliest time by which such a train could be on the rails, can be considerably shortened before even more passengers in this increasingly affluent age are lost forever to the railways.

A source of constant comment by overseas visitors, and increasingly by New Zealanders themselves, is the lack of any refreshment facilities aboard our trains. The conditions at refreshment rooms when an express pulls in are too well known to most people to require elaboration here. Not since 1917, when they were removed as a wartime economy, have dining-cars (introduced on the Christchurch expresses in 1899 by the NZR) run in regular service. The terrain over which much of the track of necessity must be built, precludes dining-cars as they are known overseas. The effect of some of the curves on a brimming bowl of soup would be little short of disastrous, and the tunnels do not allow the necessary width that a full-scale dining-car would require.

Nevertheless there seems little inherently impossible in equipping a car with some tea urns, a full-length counter, a pie-warmer and other necessities for the dispensing of refreshments en route. It is such conveniences that the railways should provide. As British Railways have so capably proved with several new trains, comfort can be just as big a travel inducement to the businessman as the greater speed of an airline. Even without swept-up stainless-steel trains, there is much that could be done to provide, not so much more comfort as more attractive travelling conditions on the passenger trains of the New Zealand Railways.

The words of the 1952 Royal Commission on the railways could perhaps be re-echoed even more pertinently today. The Commission found, for instance, that the Department's inability to provide a daytime service between Auckland and Wellington was responsible for the establishment of the Landliner bus service, estimated to have cost the Department $40,000 (in 1951) in lost potential traffic per annum. The Commission stated: "It is important therefore that a high standard of service be established . . . We do not subscribe to the view held by many people that rail passenger traffic is dying and that the whole future of the railways lies in goods haulage."

Neither with respect, does the author subscribe to this view; but more will have to be done sooner to encourage a more positive attitude on the part of the public towards the attractions and benefits of railway passenger travel.

Despite shortcomings acknowledged by even senior Departmental officers themselves, people still travel by train, though the opportunities now are very much less than they once were. The disappearance of the provincial expresses following the introduction of the 88-seat railcars has left only the Main Trunk expresses of both Islands, holiday relief trains, and the difficult-to-define Masterton-Wellington train, not accorded the dignity of the title express, but nonetheless a daily (except Saturday and Sunday) train that is in no real sense a suburban train and therefore merits inclusion in this survey.

The North Island Main Trunk is probably the best known length of railway in New Zealand. Certainly it is the most important, and every night except Saturday, when only an express runs, both the unofficially-titled Auckland Express and the officially named Night Limited run each way over this vital artery. Regrettably the passenger misses the magnificent scenery that the Main Trunk has to offer by day, and his impressions are more likely to be the lights of country towns as the train winds on through the darkness than the spectacular ravines and mountains of the central North Island. (Think of Taumarunui, for instance, at about 4 a.m. on a frosty morning, where the white glow of floodlights mingled with the sudden orange glow as fire flashed from an oilburner, steam-wreathed in the headlight of a Ka as it simmered and panted in the frosty air, sleepy passengers disembarked from the almost too-cosy heat of the carriage and the person in front who rubbed the misted window, stretched, grunted "Where the hell are we?" to his companion and recommenced his lusty snoring. These are the lingering impressions of a night on the Limited. Yet the Taumarunui country, by day, has rare beauty.)

When the Main Trunk was completed in 1909 it marked the end of an epic of engineering construction. As early as 1865 an Auckland newspaper the *Southern Cross* had said: "In the minds of a few farsighted men . . . the idea of a trunk line to Wellington did not seem a monstrous impossibility."

It was not an impossibility but from 1877, when the railway reached Frankton, until 1909, when the last section was handed over to the Railways Department, the Main Trunk had been a colossal engineering feat, involving trouble with the Maoris and the construction of viaducts, tunnels, bridges, curves, gradients, and of course the justifiably world-famous Raurimu Spiral.

Trains began running from Auckland to Wellington in 1909; old brassbound resplendent A class Pacifics hauling 200-ton trains of wooden cars ran the 426 miles in $19\frac{1}{4}$ hours with maximum permitted speeds of 40 mph. By 1914 the schedule had been reduced to $17\frac{1}{2}$ hours, and when the Ab entered the express running travelling time was reduced to $14\frac{1}{4}$ hours over the difficult line. The advent of the K and Ka class steam engines did not result in faster scheduling but it did permit train weights to be doubled within the same schedule, to some 400 tons with trains of 12-total or more.

The K and Ka engines gave splendid service on the Express and Limited and the net running time with diesel power remains the same today, only the servicing times having been eliminated. Until more powerful locomotives are obtained it seems highly unlikely that the now 13½ hour schedule will be improved upon. The Scenic Daylight however, with less stops, does the trip in 12¾ hours northbound, just over 12½ hours southbound, providing one of the most superb scenic runs it is possible to enjoy by train today. Unfortunately the Scenic Daylight runs only on Mondays and Saturdays for a short six-week season over the Christmas holidays. Considering that it has been virtually booked out every trip since 1953 when it recommenced running in its revived form (a Daylight Limited ran for a period in the summers between the two World Wars) it seems a great pity that more daylight trips are not provided on this scenically magnificent stretch of line.

In the palmy days of railway travel before the Second World War, the railways had some unique experiences to offer in the form of passenger travel that in our altered social conditions have long since disappeared. There were for instance the "Mystery Train" tours, run in the 1930s, when passengers boarded the train on a summer Sunday, and only after it had left the station, found out where they were bound for. The programmes frequently consisted of hikes, six miles along the beach or three or four through the hills, before boarding the train again for the return trip. It is somehow hard to imagine these days, being able to fill a train with people prepared to hike six miles along a beach as their Sunday entertainment. In the late twenties, it was possible to hire the Railways parlour observation car for a leisurely trip around either Island with a small party. This car was the equal of anything on rails anywhere in the world. With showers, hot and cold hand-basins, a magnificent dining-lounge with table, chairs, and sedan chairs to accommodate six, as well as sleeping facilities, it was truly a hotel on wheels.

Other more unusual passenger trains of the period were the Farmers' and Commerce Specials which toured farming or business areas of interest. These completely self-contained trains must have been the nearest thing to the Broadway Limited or Dixie Flyer that New Zealand has ever seen. The Commerce train for instance, consisted of first-class Pullmans for day accommodation, four sleeping cars, a lounge car, kitchen car, shower-bath car, and included telephones, postal service, and its own newspaper published during the four-day trip. It must have been a grand experience, and although certain enthusiast groups have since run self-contained trains on long trips, they have lacked the general standard of comfort and opulence that the Department has in the past proved it is capable of providing.

The most unusual passenger train in the country today is however unique for very different reasons than the "Golden Age" trains just mentioned. The Wairarapa's "railcar" train owes its distinction, mentioned in a previous chapter, to the fact that it replaced a railcar service, the first time in the history of the railways that the previous trend had been reversed. In the sense that its passengers are mostly commuters to the industry of the Hutt Valley and the offices of Wellington, the train is a suburban one, but as it runs over 65 miles, and starts from and returns to Masterton, in no sense a suburb of Wellington, it qualifies as a long-distance train.

A train which runs the 65 miles, with up to twelve intermediate stops, in 91 minutes, qualifies as an express in anyone's language and it appears to have the fastest average speed between any two stations a similar distance apart, of any train in the country.

Times have certainly changed from the days when the epitome of rail transport in the Valley was the old Wairarapa mail train drifting through the haze of a sweltering summer day while the heat rose and shimmered across to the brown Maungarakis and the cinders from the old A or Ab drifted in the window. The full throttle charge down the grade into the Masterton station, to grind to a halt at the platform – or as sometimes happened, to shunt sheepishly back 100 yards from the gasworks when the Ab's steam had proved better than her brakes . . . The bleating of sheep from a few wagons hitched behind the engine when an urgent consignment decreed that animals took precedence over the human passengers, and a few more minutes late wouldn't matter anyway. The old wooden cars and Abs, the soot and the steam and the leisurely progress, all have vanished into the pages of history and the memories of many.

Where once an A breasted the grade up into the Featherston Station from Pigeon Bush there now echoes the harsh beat of a diesel generator as a Da thunders over the level crossings with its trainload of workmen, tradesmen, clerks, soldiers, salesmen, office girls and a few non-regular travellers. Departing Masterton at 6.52 a.m. the six cars and van are usually soon well in tow as the Da at the head makes the easy run down the Valley, the snowcapped

Tararuas glistening in the winter sunlight, the sunscorched plains shimmering in a heat haze in the summer.

The steep grade up to the tunnel makes the speed fall but soon the engine is blasting into the hillside as the clock still wants a few minutes to 7.30 a.m. Partway through the tunnel is heard a sudden louder roar above the beat of the engine and the roaring wind, and the train has passed under the ventilation shaft that burrows 380 feet up through the rock to emerge in the Pakuratahi Valley, coincidentally right beside the formation of the old Kaitoke-Summit line. Soon the train shoots out of the tunnel as the brakes rasp on for Maymorn, where a line of old muck trucks remains from the tunnel works. On down to Upper Hutt sweeps the train, now well crowded despite the six-car capacity. As the line winds down towards the station the formation of the old Summit line can be seen to the left where it snakes its way up into the hills. Even from the brief glimpse as the train pounds into another cutting the steepness of the 1 in 35 gradients is easily appreciated.

At Upper Hutt many people get out and head towards the factories and Trentham sees the same pattern repeated as the train runs on down through the urban sprawl of the Hutt Valley, in complete contrast to the green valley dotted with grazing stock a few miles away through the hole in the hill. At 8.26 a.m. the train pulls in to Wellington and another working day for its passengers has started, until at 5.30 p.m., to the accompaniment of rustling newspapers and blaring transistors, it is time for the speedy run home.

The run home is only a few minutes slower than the mainly downhill trip, as I found when I boarded Da1488 at Featherston one evening with a typical Featherston evening zephyr threatening to blow the whole train over in a repeat performance of its successful effort with a railcar at Pigeon Bush some years previously. The train was running late due to a signal failure at Taita, and the crew lost no time in clearing Featherston to the accompaniment of the revving motor. Soon speed was picking up rapidly as we barrelled past the formation of the old branch line that many years ago ran into the tents, huts and compounds of what was once the country's largest military camp in the "war to end war".

The engine rides extremely smoothly with a virtual absence of sway as the speedo needle flicks on past the official 55 mph. The gorse is a golden blur that blends to green as well manicured paddocks flash past the thundering wheels. The welded rail makes the ride smooth and easy, only one of many constant improvements that the Railways are making all over the country. Soon Centralised Traffic Control will be installed north from Feather-ston, and New Zealand, the first nation in the world outside North America to use this tremendous signalling system, will have added yet another CTC section to the already large total of the mileage so controlled.

Past Woodside and the engine clatters out on to the Waiohine Bridge while the wind whistles around the cab window. A herd of young calves stop their frolicking for a moment to stare at the mechanical projectile flashing past and then they have vanished as the engine growls up a notch heading up the curve of the southern side of the Matarawa Bank. Soon we are rumbling down the Bank, the white needle on the speedometer swinging round into the sixties as we make up time on the best part of the track for high-speed running. At Carterton as the guard's whistle blows it's straight round into notch 8 with the sander going as the Da heaves herself up the grade out of the station. While not steep, the run up the Valley is on a general rise for most of the way, which accounts for the slightly longer time allowed for the return trip. The tablet arm goes out in readiness for the exchange at Waingawa, a bright red Da of the 1500 series waiting on the loop to cross us, the thump as the tablets are exchanged, and the rich nauseating odour of the freezing works causes us to lose no time in heading out over the Waingawa River as the water flashes by beneath us in a welter of reverberating rumbles. Stops at Solway and Renall Street see most of the few travellers still aboard disembark, and then it's the final pell-mell run down the last straight and into the station as another day in the "big smoke" ends for the Wairarapa's com-muters.

Today in the North Island the sound of express train travel is the muted throb of a diesel locomotive but the South Island, every morning except Sunday, still sees the magnificent spectacle of smoke and steam, and hears the exultant whistle that is the sound of a steam-hauled express, as the north- and southbound South Island Limited Trains 143 and 144 get under way for their 369-mile runs between Christchurch and Invercargill. The week-end night expresses between Christchurch and Dunedin, holiday relief expresses to Dunedin and the West Coast, as well as mediocre suburban trains on all but the Port Lyttelton line, are at present in the South Island normally rostered for steam.

It was on 6 September 1878 that the first through express of 10 cars and two vans hauled by the little American K class engine Washington left Christchurch at 6.07 a.m. for the first through run

to Dunedin, which was eventually reached 12½ hours later. Today
the run to Invercargill takes less time. Until 1904, two days were
required for the complete Christchurch-Invercargill journey, but in
that year a through service of 14 hours 40 minutes was instituted,
until today the South Island Limited provides a 37 mph average
over the whole trip, which includes some very difficult running
between Oamaru and Dunedin, while over the Canterbury Plains
the often 12 or more total train clips along at over 50 for many
miles.

The South Island Limited provides a service unique at present
on New Zealand trains, in that a hostess is available at all times to
provide baby's-bottle hot water, and refreshments for those too
infirm to join the scrum at the buffet – a pleasant touch of luxury
that might well be copied on other long-distance expresses. Perhaps in lighter vein the idea has certain limitations. One can
imagine a squawkbox on the side of the carriage suddenly erupting
with the preliminary burst of static, to be followed by . . . "Good
morning, ladies and gentlemen. On behalf of Guard Smith I would
like to welcome you aboard this Ja-powered Limited to Invercargill. On the footplate this morning are Driver Jones and Fireman
Brown. On behalf of New Zealand Railways may I trust you enjoy
your trip with us. Smoking is permitted but only in the cars so
reserved. When the train is in the station, please refrain from . . ."
And later: "Good morning, ladies and gentlemen, this is your
engine driver speaking. At the moment we are cruising at 50 mph
at an elevation of 159 feet. Boiler pressure is 195 lb and all signals
are green. The weather at Invercargill is misty but this is not
expected to delay us. Thank you." I think the Railways can survive
without competing to that extent! The hostess service though is a
very valuable and useful one that the Department deserves full
credit for providing.

It was Ja1270 that provided me with footplate experience of the
South Island Limited. The engine had come on at Oamaru on
the northbound train but it was at Timaru that my pass gave me
permission to make the remaining 100 miles up where the action
was. The crews had just changed as I boarded the engine, and
both driver and fireman were running their eyes over the gauges
and controls, the driver checking the running gear while the fireman banked his fire ready for the stiff climb out around Caroline
Bay. The water was topped up, the flames dancing in the grates,
the driver checking his watch, when we got the green flag sharp
on 4.31 p.m. and the Ja trembled into motion under the suppressed

M

power of the 200-lb pressure of steam shooting into the cylinders. The metallic clang of the shovel and the crisp snapping of the air-pedal-operated doors opening to the firebox rang in the cab as the engine chuffed her way around Caroline Bay while scores of holidaymakers waved her on her way. The 100 miles to Christchurch is largely easy running on straight track, and the Limited has a reputation for speed. It was going to be interesting to see how the Ja upheld the honours.

I was not disappointed. At 50 mph we were blasting our way towards Washdyke as the engine settled down to the bonejarring crashing that is a steam locomotive at speed. The fireman sportingly offered me the front half of his seat, knocking the back down for himself, and the wind plucked at my shirtsleeves as we raced on over the Plains. The fireman was keeping the front and corners of the box well supplied with coal, relying on the shaking engine to move her own fire forward in the box, and at the speed we were travelling there was no problem in this happening. As we tore away from Temuka the firebox was "chocker" and the blasting heat burst into the cab as the doors banged open to receive yet more fuel. The noise of the engine is tremendous; the whole cab shakes and rattles as if determined to tear itself loose from the boiler, the exhaust thunders in a staccato so rapid it is almost one continuous sound, the injector surges as it thumps on, the generator howls its banshee note, the shovel clangs, the wheels bang, as at 65 mph the whole living, breathing, shouting piece of machinery bellows along like an Apache on the warpath.

Having realised that I was no novice to fast steam engine riding by the fact that I was not kneeling in prayer for deliverance from this madhouse nor hanging on with whitened knuckles and ashen face, the crew soon gave me the opportunity to prove my worth. The Sellars injector was no problem; by now I knew the trick of partially opening the valve, holding it for a second or two, and then releasing it fully to hear the satisfying rumble of water passing into the boiler. But firing was a bit different. My past experience had hitherto been confined to Abs or Js at 30 mph and now I was being given the opportunity on the bouncing deck of a Ja at 60. The pedal that activates the doors is about 3 inches wide and 15 inches long, not such a very large target when the deck is going up and down like a rowboat in Cook Strait. As well as consciously directing my hands with the shovel, my left foot had to be carefully placed and on top of trying to merely keep upright without support, it was nowhere near as easy as the grinning fireman made it seem.

Fortunately I managed to hit the pedal, and the coal shot into the gaping red mouth of the box as I got into the swing that was by now fairly familiar. There was one nasty moment when I lifted my foot too soon and the doors snapped on the shovel like a hungry barracuda, but fortunately nothing worse happened and the coal kept banging in as sweat began to trickle down my nose from the heat and effort. Satisfyingly black smoke, the sign that the fresh coal has caught, came welling out of the stack as I gained the refuge of the seat again while the whole outfit thundered madly on.

The job wasn't over yet, though. Lumps of coal glared accusingly at me from the floor as I hastened to grab the handbrush and sweep them in front of the backhead before picking them up on the shovel. Waste not want not; besides, it made it a lot easier underfoot. A splash around with the hose removed the fine dust and grit and, when sloshed over into the bunker, brought quick relief from the flying coal specks and dust dislodged by the wind of our passage and the heat of the air.

At maximum cut-off (minimum steam), and with the regulator only half open we swept over the Rangitata Bridge and steadily increased speed. The Jas have a reputation for fast running, and have previously been quoted as able to run freely at speeds in the region of 75 mph with a full train. I am happy to confirm their reputation. With a train of well over 350 tons and the throttle only half open we were steaming along with the speedo needle well into the seventies. It was exhilarating, to say the least of it. The big engine was fairly whipping along, the smoke streaming back over the train as the slipstream screamed past the racing engine.

What on earth, I wondered incredulously, could she do on *full* throttle? If this experience was only half throttle I was prepared to believe the stories I had heard from drivers of 80 and 90 mph running with the Ja. Such plus 70 mph performances are even more impressive when it is realised that they are given in ordinary service conditions, on narrow gauge track, and with an engine whose driving wheel diameter of 4 feet 6 inches falls far short of the 6 feet or more considered necessary overseas for such performances. Ja1270 certainly lived up to the last two digits in her number.

For miles on end the incredible pace continued. Bucking, rocking, swaying or perhaps it was merely prancing, the Ja hurtled her train along at consistently high speeds, and the station agent at Hinds waving us through was a mere blur as we sped on before having, reluctantly it seemed on the locomotive's part, to slow for some light track that would not permit such fast running. At 5.59, some four minutes late due to a delay at the station, we pulled out of Ashburton, and there was some more spirited running to Rakaia where we made an unscheduled stop at the signal to allow a southbound railcar to scuttle on to the loop out of our way. The welded rail again gave the Ja the opportunity to show her paces, though with less free rein than she had previously been enjoying, and she howled majestically up the Bankside grade to continue on at an effortlessly maintained 55 to keep her to time.

I was still working the injector and keeping an eye on the water-level. Too much, and anything can happen — cylinders blown, a jammed injector, or a sudden stop with a full boiler and the water surge will force water to erupt out of the stack.

The grade up out of Burnham kept speed to 40 mph but 1270, besides being fleet of foot, could pull like a plough horse if need be and treated such matters as grades with the sheer contempt of a free-running thoroughbred. Such impetuous and vigorous running unfortunately could not last for ever, and after a steady slowing through the suburbs as I heaved in my last scoop of coal and gave her one last shot of the injector under the supervising eye of the fireman, we clanked slowly into Christchurch Station smack on time. After uncoupling, we ran slowly off down to the huge depot at Linwood, where no less than 56 steam engines of five different classes are based, and left 1270 to the attention of the shed crew.

The New Zealand Railways, so frequently referred to as snailways or cited Biblically (Gen. 1, v. 25 "And God made . . . everything that creepeth upon the earth . . .") by those with no real knowledge of the frequently tortuous track over which the trains are obliged to run, had certainly proved that, given good track, the old NZR can hoof it with the best of overseas railways.

18

The end draws near

B Y THE TIME these words appear in print, it seems most
unlikely that there will be any steam locomotives at work in
the North Island, while those in the South will at best have
only a few more years of work allotted to them.

In many ways other than mere sentimentality this situation is to
be regretted. New Zealand has a long and a proud tradition of
steam locomotive building and our New Zealand-designed and
built steam engines have been justifiably world-famous. To the
man in the street accustomed in the majority of cases to viewing
the railways with something akin to a sneer, let it be firmly understood that the steam locomotives of the New Zealand Railways
were in world class. Particularly in the final stages of steam development, the J and K classes (all sentiment aside) were magnificent
examples of the steam locomotive builder's art, and their passing
brings to an end the great age of steam power in New Zealand.

Like many another saga, the beginnings were fairly humble.
Pilgrim, No 1 of the Canterbury Provincial Government's railways,
chuffed her way to fame as the first steam engine in the country
with the opening of the first railway in the Colony on 1 December
1863. A very "British" styled locomotive, Pilgrim was imported
from Victoria to work on the 5 foot 3 inch gauge railways of
Canterbury.

The broad-gauge engines soon established an enviable reputation for fast running over the Canterbury Plains. Several instances
are on record. On one occasion medical assistance had to be rushed
out from Christchurch to Rolleston, the driver being asked to lose
no speed on the way. He covered the 14 miles in 13 minutes, and
his fireman, when not firing, reportedly sat on the cab floor clinging
to the brake pedestal as the engine rocketed along at 65 mph.
There were also several unofficial attempts to see if the 6 miles 64
chains from Rangiora to Kaiapoi could be clocked in the even
seven minutes, until the management came to hear of things —

after which the attempted record-setting came to a sudden halt! The speed and efficiency of the broad-gauge engines were far superior to the smaller narrow-gauge engines that followed them, built for low speeds on track constructed to the least possible incidence of expenditure.

The 3 foot 6 inch gauge engines of the early days all suffered from the economy of Julius Vogel's Public Works Policy, and for many years the light little engines were scathingly contrasted with their larger predecessors by both public and engineers alike. Until 1877 the railways had relied on the smaller tank engines of the F, A, C, D, and G classes, as well as the interesting single and double Fairlie's Patent type, with their driving-wheels swivelling on a bogie. These tank and articulated engines were ideal for much of the traffic prevailing on the narrow curves of the early lines when speed was usually impossible anyway on such restricted track.

The F class 0-6-0 tank in particular was a most useful engine, and although first built in 1872, the last did not leave Government rails until 1966, and at least one is still employed on private rails, in itself a remarkable tribute. They were regularly employed as shunting engines in their latter years until the advent of widespread dieselisation of shunting services in the 1950s, but unfortunately they did not grow to keep pace with the wagons they shunted. When coupled to a box wagon in later years, their crews had to defy gravity and lean far out of the cab to be able to see the shunter's signals, while almost having to work the regulator with one foot. There can be little doubt however that they were the first really successful class of engine on the railways, and as such were the forerunners of many other famous engines of later days. The only tender engine introduced in this period was the 2-6-0 type J used mainly for goods work.

Over the next few years, beginning in 1878, the dashing K, Q, and T classes were introduced from America, the K having the honour of pulling the first Christchurch-Dunedin express. The old T class 2-8-0 "consolidations" which arrived in 1879 were right out of the pages of a *Harper's Weekly* or *Police Gazette* feature on the famous Denver and Rio Grande Railroad. With stubby wheels, enormous oil lamps, diamond stacks, ornate wooden cabs and tea-caddy sand-domes they were, even from the faded brown tints of an old photograph, wonderfully picturesque little engines. These Yankee classes were followed by English 2-6-2 and 2-8-0 engines classified V and P respectively, with similar N and O classes from the Baldwin Locomotive Works of Philadelphia, builders of the earlier American engines. There was considerable controversy at the time in the Colony over the respective merits of English and American engines, but in 1889 an event occurred which was to lead eventually to the argument being nothing more than an academic exercise.

In that year the W class tank engine was built at Addington Workshops, the New Zealand Railways' first effort at locomotive building. In essence it was little more than a rebuilt tank version of the earlier J class, but it is of historic importance as the first Railways Department-designed and built steam engine, the forerunner of many eminently successful local designs. It was to be some years however before the New Zealand workshops could do much towards a locomotive building programme, handicapped as they were by staff shortages and lack of facilities. Notable designs being developed or purchased however included the U class 4-6-0s, and the various W class tank engines, the Wa, Wb, Wd, We – curiously, there never was a Wc class engine! In 1901, one of several New Zealand Railways' "firsts", the 4-6-2 Q class made its appearance, to become world-famous as the first locomotives of their wheel arrangement (termed "Pacific") in the world. From this 4-6-2 arrangement have developed fast passenger and general duties locomotives, in use all over the world. The world steam speed record holder Mallard (126 mph) of the British Railways, was a Pacific locomotive.

It was about this period that the Railways began to place in service engines many of which, at the time of writing, are still working though almost exclusively confined to the South Island. Among such engines are the Wf class 4-6-4 tanks, two of which may still be seen at Greymouth; the Ww class tank engines; and the famous A class compound Pacifics, forerunners of a long line of A, Aa, and Ab class compound and simple locomotives. The A class engines are still at work occasionally in Southland and on the West Coast, a far cry from the days when they proudly wheeled expresses over many sections of NZR tracks. The A was considered by many drivers to be a better engine off the mark than was the later Ab. With a smaller firebox they were not as easy to fire; but when in good order they were fine steaming locomotives, particularly after they had been warmed up with several miles' running, and the driver of an A could expect great things. It was essential for the fireman to keep the back corners of the box well filled, otherwise it could be extremely difficult to get steam up, but generally they were a popular locomotive with crews, particularly after they were converted to more normal simple two-cylinder engines. Their main drawback was a tendency to rough riding and and in later years, when one of the few fast services they still worked was the Wairarapa's school train from Cross Creek, though the As maintained the tight schedule they were never as popular at this stage of their careers as the newer Abs.

In 1899, the first of the B class 4-8-0 goods engines appeared and were followed in 1911 by the slightly modified Ba. The B class are powerful engines for all their modest size, and until a few years ago were the mainstay of the Reefton section while also handling loads up to Otira. Originally narrow firebox engines, several Bs and Bas were reboilered with wide fireboxes which gave them a new lease of life. Somewhat stubby engines, they seemed with their little 42½-inch driving-wheels and high boilers, to be all boiler, which gave them an appearance of tremendous power. They were obviously built for slow, heavy haulage. The B and Ba engines were never very popular with firemen, the narrow firebox engines in particular being very difficult to fire. Only a couple of scoops at a time could usually be tossed in, otherwise they simply clogged up. There was little need for a fireman's seat; "little and often" was the firing rule. Until recently a B could still be seen thrashing its way up the 1 in 25 of the Blackball Mine branch, the fireman working like an automaton to keep up the steam, but with the recent closure of this branch it appears unlikely that the West Coast Bs will see regular line service again, though a few still work shunts at Dunedin. Another of New Zealand's steam veterans will have passed on.

As a 1914 development of these classes came the Bb, an engine designed primarily for freight and mixed traffic duties, with the then high tractive effort of some 22,000 lb at 85 per cent working pressure. For many years these game little engines struggled along with 700-ton goods trains but they were eventually relegated to shunt and branch line duties. They worked the Glen Afton, Foxton, and Motuhora branches as well as performing sterling yard service in their declining years, notably at Palmerston North and Frankton. They were however a fairly rugged engine to work on, it was often said of them: "A fortnight on a Bb and a fortnight in hospital." Stories of their rough riding were legendary; one new shunt driver taking over a Bb was twice, in the first quarter hour, alleged to have slapped on emergency and jumped from his cab to count the number of wheels he felt sure must have fallen off – until he realised it was only the old Bb leaping every time she went over a wide rail joint!

Despite the excellent work of the B classes, however, the giants of the early twentieth century freight runs were the beautifully massive X class compound engines first built in 1906. These husky brutes were masters of their work. They hauled 900 tons on level track, only 100 less than the considerably later K classes and more than the modern J and Ja locomotives can handle. During the early 1940s, 11 of the X class were converted to four-cylinder simple engines, with their tractive effort increased to 30,000 lb. In later years they worked mainly in the Taumarunui, Stratford, and Gisborne-Napier areas, but they were never popular with the crews that worked them.

They had given wonderful service in the past and gave good service when regular men ran them, but the trouble really began when engines were "pooled". The failures became frequent, even among the simple engines. During the war an "X roster" had been worked at Taumarunui, and with regular crews who were prepared to spend often considerable hours of their spare time maintaining them they gave faithful service. They were heavy engines on water, and could drain the tender in 25 miles with even a moderate load. By the 1950s, shortly before they were scrapped, they were hated by most crews who had anything to do with them, but it must be remembered that they were difficult engines to maintain, particularly at a time when staff was at a premium; apart from their reputed distinction of being the first 4-8-2 engines in the world, they will be remembered as the first of the "big" steamers.

In 1915 there came to the New Zealand railway scene what must undoubtedly rank as the finest all-round New Zealand-designed engine that ever turned a wheel on the nation's tracks: the famous Ab, a legend in its lifetime, still performing great feats of haulage, and without a doubt the most popular engine with crews, ever to run on the New Zealand Railways. Time and again I have heard drivers acclaim the merits of the Ab, in tones of very real warmth and respect. To all who knew them they were, and are, a wonderful engine.

The Ab was the successor to the A class, but it was a two-cylinder simple engine, and proved its superiority over its predecessor in a series of dramatic tests in 1916. It could haul more cars at a faster speed with greater economy of fuel and water than the A was capable of. Officially recorded speeds for an Ab range up to 66·5 mph with 385 tons trailing. They were the most ubiquitous class of engine on the railways, 141 being built, with 11 more added as rebuilds from the Wab tank engine version. Truly excellent all-rounders, they handled passenger trains up to 400 tons and goods trains of up to 750 tons in easy country.

It is not difficult to understand the great popularity they enjoyed with engine crews. There was not a single bad steamer in the whole class and while some were better than others, as a class they were excellent steaming engines. They were clean and easy to fire, and more than one fireman has told me: "It's a pleasure to fire these engines." The Ab is an extremely comfortable engine to ride in, singularly free from much of the jolting and bouncing that other classes were often prone to. The cab is quite spacious for an engine of relatively modest dimensions, not too hot and fairly smoke-free. Other engines have been bigger and faster, newer and more powerful, but of the many hundreds of miles of footplate travel I have undertaken on many different classes of engines, those miles in the cabs of Abs have been in many ways the most pleasant.

Confined nowadays to goods and mixed trains, the Abs still give sterling service, and on enthusiast specials they have frequently shown the silver heels of their bygone express days, when a train of red wooden cars, the black boiler gleaming in contrast to the bright brass bands on the sand-domes, and the flashing silver links of the coupling rods, was a sight to excite the mind and gladden the eye of anyone with an appreciation of manmade beauty. In a few years the last Ab will be retired — I sincerely hope not to vanish completely; but it is safe to say that the memory of the Ab will be evergreen in the minds of all who knew these remarkable and beautiful engines.

If the success of the Ab was total, the only word that could be applied to New Zealand's sole venture (1928) into the world of the Beyer-Garratt articulated locomotives is "abysmal". These articulated engines with their boilers slung between the two sets of wheels have enjoyed tremendous success in Africa and Australia, but basically New Zealand was not ready for them, and after much trouble with their valve gear, the mechanical stokers, and sundry other mechanical failures, they were in 1937 cut up into six G class Pacific engines. It is doubtful whether, with the possible exception of Pearson's Dream, there was ever a more unpopular class of engine on the railways. They provided some eloquent copy in the *Locomotive Engineers' Journal*. They were stationed at Christchurch and Springfield, to the constant loathing of crews unfortunate enough to have to work them: "Any depot that has the misfortune to have these six mechanical abortions wished on them has our deepest sympathy," wrote one scribe in the *Journal*.

Their normal running condition seemed to be for the whole front to be obscured in steam, and on a frosty morning at Springfield, a G getting a train away was a sight to unnerve the most stalwart of men. They were described by one driver who worked on them as "triple barrelled, double opposed, anti-clockwise fog generators. They went in leaps and bounds like a constipated kangaroo with double hernia and had a charming habit of suddenly converting themselves from three to two cylinder engines if you allowed them to drift too long."

Finally, in what must have been an historic release, the General Manager stated in 1956: "It has been decided not to carry out any further repairs on the G locomotives and I am pleased to say that arrangements have been made for them to be permanently 'stopped'." The rejoicing was universal and, unlamented, the terrible Gs were booted rather than bowed off the NZR.

Despite the setback with the Garratts and their New Zealand-built G class offspring, the setback emphasised rather than detracted from the generally outstanding success of New Zealand-designed and built steam locomotives of the twentieth century. As the traffic built up and became increasingly difficult for the Abs to handle, there appeared in 1932 the first of the massive and magnificent K class that heralded the final great period of steam power for the New Zealand Railways.

The K was described in 1950 by an American railroad authority as "easily the best-designed locomotive operating on this [3 ft 6 in] gauge to be found anywhere ... They steam freely, ride smoothly and curve extremely well ..."

For over a quarter of a century they, together with the Ka, were the backbone of the North Island railway system. Designed to the requirements of P. R. Angus, Chief Mechanical Engineer, who also gave the New Zealand Railways the Ka, Kb, J and Ja classes, railcars, Ed and Ds engines, they were beautifully proportioned, powerful 4-8-4 mixed-traffic locomotives rated for 500-ton expresses and 1,000-ton goods trains. They were large engines, and the fire grate area of 47·7 square feet was, as earlier mentioned, reputedly the largest handfired grate on any locomotive in the world. They were certainly capable of hauling the traffic, though it was tough work on the fireman, and after their conversion to oilburners, beginning in 1946, their popularity with the man in the left-hand seat increased enormously.

By 1953 when coal was becoming cheaper and more plentiful, it was decided to reconvert the class back to coal. Consternation reigned among North Island crews – to the mild amusement of men still firing the South Island Kbs, which have always been coalburners, and the move was accompanied by violent outbursts from the locomotive men. The first to be reconverted was No 915.

After her return from the shops she was banished to the back-shunt at Frankton and immediately lost one or two vital parts to other Ks, to effectively keep her immobile and ensure that the oilburners were kept on the road at her expense! The staff shortage was then acute, and the locomotive men had visions of their already thin ranks being further depleted by the mass resignation of a generation of firemen reared on oilburners. The situation eventually was reached that the union instructed men not to work 915, and also 901 and 925 which had meantime been reconverted. Before the testing point was reached, oil prices fell and the three engines were converted back to oil again.

Over the years, the Ks underwent many minor external changes, including the unusual fitting of the headlight into a recess on the top of the smokebox, a change which did nothing technically or aesthetically to improve the engine, but which became the K's main obvious distinction from the Ka. The introduction of main line diesels set the seal on the fate of the Ks, and they were gradually withdrawn, until 911, the sole survivor, left the NZR in the latter half of 1966. The K was a great achievement and a credit to the Railways Department; it was highly successful right from the outset, compared extremely well in terms of power rating with many overseas engines, and carved an impressive niche in the history of locomotive development in New Zealand.

The most triumphant note of steam in the North Island was sounded by the thunderous bellow and full-throated whistle of the Ka (the 1939 development of the K), 35 of which were built between 1939 and 1950. To me, the Ka remains the most impressive locomotive I have ever come in contact with. In my travels I have noticed that the Ab is spoken of by drivers with affection; the Da with an impersonal respect; but the Ka in tones of respectful awe as befitted what was a truly great locomotive.

Exercising over 32,000 lb of tractive effort at 85 per cent of the working pressure, weighing 145 tons in working trim, they were good-sized engines by any standard, and on the 3 foot 6 inch gauge of New Zealand lines they looked exactly what they were, powerful brutish engines, equally at ease with a 25 mph goods train as a 60 mph express. They were rated to pull 550 tons at 30 mph on mountain grades, or 1,000 tons on the flat, and they easily wheeled expresses of 400 tons over the Makerua Plains at a regular 55-60 mph. Like the Ks, originally coalburners, they were converted from 1947 onwards to burn fuel oil.

As coalburners, they were not popular with firemen, being very dusty engines, and the fireman on a mountain run would be expected to shovel 2½ tons or more of coal in two hours and be lucky if he sat down twice the whole time. The draught on the Ka was such that it would burn practically anything, and skilful firing was not so necessary as simply heaving coal anyhow into the roaring fire. This was a fault in the view of a fireman who had been proud of having to use care and skill in banking his fire. With the conversion to oilburners (the last two of the class, Nos 958 and 959, were built as oilburners) the fireman's job, as with the K, became less strenuous. As oilburners they were a very popular locomotive with crews, steaming well and always having strength in reserve when the occasion demanded.

Despite a tender capacity of 7½ tons of coal and 5,000 gallons of water, or 1,500 gallons of fuel oil and 5,000 gallons of water as oilburners, the Kas were both hungry and thirsty engines when they had to cope with a grade. On flat runs, with a light train, a Ka burned some four gallons of fuel oil per mile; on mountain grades this doubled to about eight gallons per mile. In the 45 miles from Marton to Taihape, which is on an average grade of 1 in 100 for the 15 miles to Hunterville and 1 in 70 for the remaining 30 miles to Taihape, a Ka with a 400-ton train guzzled something like 3,750 gallons of water, or 83 gallons per mile.

Over the years the Kas have put up some remarkable performances on the difficult Main Trunk track. For sheer speed on easy track they leave a Da standing, and on difficult sections of track with a passenger train, Kas have often recorded better times with similar trains than their diesel rivals. A peak speed of 69 mph with a 200-ton train has been officially recorded; other unofficial speeds range into the 70s.

In all honesty I doubt if anyone really knows what speed a Ka in first class order could have reached, for the track has never really permitted them to go all out. I have been quoted speeds of 90 with the Limited and, knowing the engine and the driver concerned, I have no reason to doubt this. Perhaps it can best be summed up in the words of another driver: "Speed? God knows, I reckon they'd hit the 'ton' if we could really open them up."

Isolated record type speeds, however spectacular, are of course no substitute for steady day-to-day averages, but the Kas never gave any cause for complaint in the average day-to-day running of a railway. They have hauled goods trains, mixed trains, passenger trains, in the wintry blast of a Waiouru snowstorm and the subtropical heat of an Auckland summer, across the Shannon Flats and the gruelling incompensated 1 in 50 of the Raurimu Spiral, and they have proved time and again, that they were one of the most outstanding locomotive classes that this country has ever seen.

The final development of steam locomotion is found in the J classes, designed again by Mr Angus, and built initially by the North British Locomotive Company. The J was intended for use on lighter secondary main line track for which the K classes were too weighty. The original Js were a most handsome locomotive, with their torpedo-nosed streamline cowling, one of the few aesthetically successful applications of streamlining to steam locomotives, in my opinion, in the world. From 1947 however, the cowling was removed to facilitate maintenance. Twelve of the original 40 Js were converted to oilburners and reclassified Jb and, among other spheres of operations, they handled for many years all the traffic on the Stratford-Okahukura line.

The final development of the J was the Ja class, of two types: the Hillside-built coalburning engines used in the South Island, and the 1952 oilburning Jas built for Auckland area service by the North British Locomotive Company. All variations of the J class have been fairly popular engines with the men who worked them. On expresses they were reckoned to be only half as hard to work as the aging Abs, and they were generally fairly good steaming engines, riding well, but often tending to be excessively hot in the cab.

Some of the crews on the West Coast however appear to have mixed feelings towards the J classes now making their presence felt on the Otira section. While the J on this run generally shows better pick-up and has more punch, it does not hold steam as well as an Ab. Some firemen have even gone as far as to say that a good Ab was often as good as a J. Whether the conversion to hard coal made any difference is hard to say.

When in North Island use, the J had cyclone patent fittings in the smokebox to increase the draught, but with Coast coal only a spark arrestor is fitted. North Island crews generally thought the J an excellent pulling locomotive when in its prime, though the Jb was considered by some to be not as good a steamer after conversion to oilfiring.

I have travelled on Js, Jas, and Jbs, and generally found them all very capable locomotives, though tending to have an end-to-end sidesway to the detriment of their riding qualities. On the West Coast they are rated for 420 tons up the difficult climb to Otira, and have made a considerable difference to the previous A and Ab workings. The South Island Jas, in particular, on the racetracks between Timaru and Christchurch, have proved excellent locomotives, with running speeds of 75 mph and more being mentioned on occasion, an extremely impressive speed indeed with relatively small driving-wheels and on narrow-gauge track. The Ja-hauled South Island Limited has now the distinction of being the only regularly scheduled daily (except Sunday) steam-hauled train in the country and when diesels inevitably replace steam it will be most interesting to see whether the magnificent Ja performances can even be equalled in speed and easy running ability.

An impressive, slim-looking, almost lithe locomotive, the Ja, last steam engine class to be built for the New Zealand Railways, is an impressive achievement. Thoroughly modern, with roller bearings, Baker valve gear noted for its accurate steam distribution over long periods, coupled with easy maintenance, the Ja represents the technological limit of the steam locomotive in this country. That they have only a few more years of work allowed them is to be very much regretted. They are a fit engine to enjoy the distinction of being the last in a proud tradition of locomotive construction and operation.

The last days of steam locomotive operation are giving increasing emphasis to the question of preservation. Fortunately, when the last steam engine is retired from the New Zealand Railways, that will not be the end of steam in New Zealand. Dedicated groups of enthusiasts are doing much to ensure that the great heritage of steam is not lost.

Two such schemes deserving of special praise are the Ocean Beach Railway at Dunedin, already an operating steam museum, and the Christchurch Ferrymead Railway which, when completed, will operate several large steam engines on the line of track on which New Zealand's first railway was formed; a more fitting site could not be imagined.

The Bush Tramway Club in the North Island intends also to operate a steam-worked museum track. This is preservation in its ultimate. When one sees at Taumarunui the rusting hulk of the old W that pulled the Parliamentary special at the opening of the Main Trunk, or Opossum, a little A class 0-4-0 tank engine built in Wellington in 1875 and now half rusted away at Greymouth, one doubts the value of such preservation. Engines which are part of this country's history, which were working machines, deserve better than to rust away in a children's playground. Fortunately, not all engines have been so neglected; the immaculately painted Fell 199 at Featherston probably looks better now than when she first rolled from the workshops, but not all are in this happy state.

It is a matter of personal regret to me that the Railways Department has not considered preserving one or two engines in operating order, as has been done on several of the American railroads, where steam excursions, with a surcharge paid to a maintenance fund, have proved that this can be done without financial loss. In Britain too, private steam locomotives have been given certain running rights over British Railways tracks, a state of affairs at present not permitted in this country. But this is in no way to disparage what the Department has already done. It has donated engines for preservation and has itself preserved a handful of older engines, unfortunately not generally on public display; and it has also made old track and some vehicles available to preservation societies.

While it is appreciated that engines have a considerable scrap value, many private firms responsible to their shareholders have donated engines in running order to preservation schemes. A Ka or Ab in running order would be worth immensely more as a preservation gift than a dozen engines sitting forlornly on concrete blocks to rust away, forgotten and lifeless. British Railways, hardly renowned for their operating profits in the last 20 years, maintain a transport museum of locomotives in immaculate order. It would be a wonderful thing for railway enthusiasts and for the cause of our nation's historical record, if the Railways Department were able to take an even more active interest in the preservation of locomotives that have worked for the country, and for the Railways themselves, so well for so long. It is still not too late.

Steam engines have served New Zealand well for over 100 years. A product of the best influences in British and American locomotive design, with in later years a predominance of the latter, New Zealand-designed and built locomotives evolved to a style all their own and they have been outstandingly successful on the difficult grades and curves that abound on New Zealand lines.

All too soon they will be only a memory. To the men who fired them, drove them, at times cursed them — and, in a gruff manner, loved them; and to the enthusiast whose pulse quickened at their vibrant exhaust and piercing whistle, the New Zealand Railways will be the poorer for their passing.

Their epitaph is to be found in the words of St Matthew's Gospel, Chapter 25 Verse 21: Well done, thou good and faithful servant.

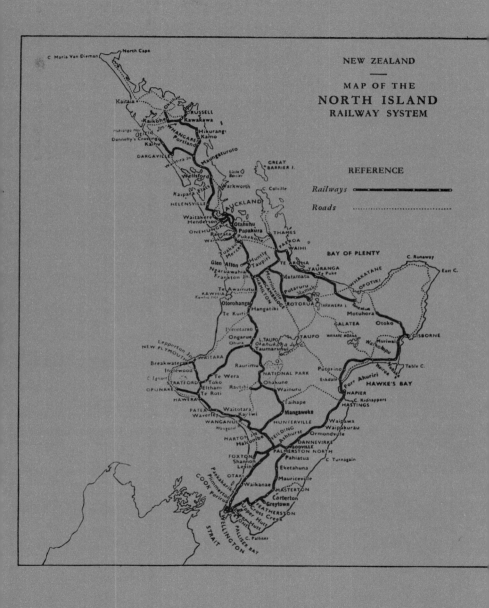

NEW ZEALAND
—
MAP OF THE
NORTH ISLAND
RAILWAY SYSTEM

REFERENCE

Railways
Roads